A DISCUSSION ON THE SYSTEM OF SOCIALISM WITH CHINESE CHARACTERISTICS

HE YITING

Translated by
MARTIN WARD

ACA PUBLISHING LTD

ACA Publishing Ltd
University House
11-13 Lower Grosvenor Place,
London SW1W 0EX, UK
Tel: +44 20 3289 3885
E-mail: info@alaincharlesasia.com
www.alaincharlesasia.com

Author: He Yiting
Translator: Martin Ward

**Published by ACA Publishing Ltd in association with People's
Publishing House**

Original Chinese Text © 论中国特色社会主义制度 *(Lùn zhōngguó tèsè
shèhuì zhǔyì zhìdù)* 2020, People's Publishing House, Beijing China

English Translation text © 2022 ACA Publishing Ltd, London, UK

Paperback ISBN: 978-1-83890-007-6
eBook ISBN: 978-1-83890-007-6

A catalogue record for *A Discussion on the System of Socialism with Chinese
Characteristics* is available from the National Bibliographic Service of the British
Library.

CONTENTS

PREFACE

The nine essays in this booklet represent what I have learnt and come to understand since the Fourth Plenary Session of the 19th CPC Central Committee and have all been previously presented publicly. These articles revolve around one topic, namely, guided by Xi Jinping Thought on Socialism with Chinese Characteristics for a New Era, evaluating the theoretical contribution, practical achievements and distinct advantages of socialism with Chinese characteristics in order to increase the confidence of the readers in this system. Critical evaluation of this booklet is most welcome.

He Yiting
    December 2019

CHAPTER ONE

THE SUPERIORITY OF SOCIALISM WITH CHINESE CHARACTERISTICS

Socialism with Chinese characteristics is an advanced and distinctively Chinese system possessing significant institutional advantages and a strong intrinsic capacity for self-improvement. This system provides a fundamental institutional guarantee for the Chinese nation to usher in a great leap from standing up and getting rich to becoming strong. The central key in China's governance is China's systems and institutions.

The type of national system a country chooses is determined by that country's historical heritage, cultural traditions, and level of economic and social development, and is also determined by the people of the country.

Socialism with Chinese characteristics was born and has grown from China's long political and cultural traditions, from her struggles against foreign aggression, for national independence and for the liberation of her people since the mid-19th century, as well as from the arduous establishment and hard-fought exploration of the socialist cause. This system constitutes a great innovation by the CPC and the Chinese people, and also a great innovation in the history of human institutions and civilisation.

The creativity of this system lies in the fact that it constitutes the creative practice of the Marxist Theory of Social Formation in China, and the concretisation of the theory of scientific socialism at the institutional level, as well as being the manifestation of the achievement of the socialist system in China. The whole path of socialism from theory to practice and then on to its implementation in numerous countries and its development all the way to the present day demonstrates that the socialist system constitutes the unity of general form and special forms.

The principle of the general form of the socialist system has been scientifically answered by classic writers such as Marx, Engels and Lenin. This general form can only be reflected through the socialist system of each specific country and is realistic only if it is presented in a specific ethnic or national form or specific era. In other words, there is no, and can be no, unified model for the implementation of socialism suitable for the situation of every country. The only approach is to integrate the basic principles of scientific socialism with the actual and era-specific characteristics of each country, follow a socialist road which conforms to the country's specific national conditions, and establish a socialist system which embodies the country's unique characteristics. As Comrade Deng Xiaoping pointed out: "The integration of the universal truths of Marxism-Leninism with the concrete reality of the country - this in itself constitutes a universal truth."

The creativity of this system lies in the fact that it is a scientific system formed by the Chinese people led by the CPC during the process of the long-term practical exploration of revolution, construction and reform. In the course of revolution, construction and reform, in accordance with the basic principles of Marxism, the CPC started from an acknowledgement of China's national conditions, mustered the wisdom and strength of the people, and continued to construct a scientific, standardised and stable system, providing institutional safeguards and support for China's development. After the founding of new China and the establishment of the institution of the NPC, multi-party cooperation and political consultation under the leadership of the CPC laid the institutional foundations for the Chinese nation to move from standing up and becoming more prosperous to becoming stronger. Since reform and opening up, China's national institutions and national system of governance have been continuously improved through the reform and innovations of various institutional mechanisms.

Socialism with Chinese characteristics consists of a set of systems and institutions which constitute a rigorous, complete and systematically integrated system, including the system of party leadership, systems and institutions that ensure the people are the masters of the country, the socialist rule of law system with Chinese characteristics, the socialist system of governance with Chinese characteristics, the basic socialist economic system, the advanced socialist cultural system, systems protecting people's livelihoods, the system of social governance, the system of eco-civilisation, the system of the absolute leadership of the party over the PLA, institutions sustaining "One Country, Two Systems", the system of foreign affairs, and the system of party and state supervision and so on. Within the system of socialism with Chinese characteristics, the fundamental institutions, the basic institutions and the major institutions play the fundamental structural role of "Four Beams and Eight Pillars", and the institution with the most dominant position therein is the system of party leadership. All the work and activities of China's national governance are conducted in accordance with the system of socialism with Chinese characteristics, forming a national system of governance and governability which covers all aspects and sectors, ensuring the normal operation of national and social life. The innovative aspect of this system is that it is a Chinese blueprint provided by the CPC to seek out a better social system for mankind.

Some people in the West believe that the Western system is the only option for achieving modernisation and a universal institutional model. End-of-history theorists claim that capitalist liberal democracy constitutes the "end of the evolution of human ideology" and the "last form of human domination". The undertakings of new China over the past 70 years have demonstrated a truth to the world: The Western institutional model is not the only way to govern and modernise a country; in fact, every country can walk its own path. Every country and every nation has the right to choose a system suited to them and to pioneer a path to modernisation marked by the features of that country. The great success of socialism with Chinese characteristics provides strong proof of this.

Comrade Xi Jinping's book *The Governance of China*, and the strengths of socialism with Chinese characteristics thereby revealed, have shown to the world the diversity of available paths to modernisation, the richness of human civilisation and the range of options for national institutions and systems of national governance, providing developing countries with new options for routes to modernisation.

SOCIALISM WITH CHINESE CHARACTERISTICS POSSESSES TREMENDOUS STRENGTHS

In order to discern whether a system is good or possesses strengths, it is necessary to evaluate and grasp the situation surrounding the big picture from a political perspective, and mainly observe whether said system conforms with national conditions, functions effectively, and is supported by the people. Or, in other words, the only way to find out if a shoe fits is by trying it on. There are no two identical models of political system in the entire world, and a political system cannot be abstractly evaluated in isolation from specific social and political conditions and historical and cultural traditions. Furthermore, it is even less appropriate to rigidly apply a foreign political model in another country.

Socialism with Chinese characteristics is a national system possessing many significant advantages. In a key speech at the conference celebrating the 60th anniversary of the founding of the NPC, Comrade Xi Jinping proposed the standards of the "Eight Whethers" for assessing a political system, stating:

"[The criteria required] for evaluating whether or not a country's political system is democratic and effective are mainly whether or not the leadership of the country can transition in an orderly manner in accordance with the law, whether or not the people can manage state and social affairs and economic and cultural undertakings in accordance with the law, whether or not the people can freely express their interests, whether or not all sections of society can participate effectively in the political life of the country, whether or not national decision-making can be achieved scientifically and democratically, whether or not all kinds of talented individuals can enter the national leadership and management systems by way of fair competition, whether or not the ruling party can achieve leadership in state affairs in accordance with the provisions of the Constitution, and whether or not effective control and supervision can be implemented in the exercising of authority."

The remarkable advantages of socialism with Chinese characteristics concisely summarised from 13 aspects by the Fourth Plenary Session of the 19th CPC Central Committee embodied the metric of the "Eight Whethers" and proved that socialism with Chinese characteristics is a practicable, truly efficacious and efficient system.

Among the 13 obvious advantages of socialism with Chinese characteristics, what is extremely important is that the CPC unites the development of the correct road, the development of scientific theory and the construction of an effective system, guides the construction of the national system using Sinicised Marxism and developing Marxism, and transforms the experience of successful application into results at an institutional level in a timely manner, so that China's national system not only embodies the basic principles of scientific socialism, but also possesses distinct Chinese characteristics, national characteristics and characteristics representative of the times. It is also very important that this system never excludes any other country's experience of governance beneficial for China's development and progress, but it is broad-minded, upholds a China-centred approach, keeps what is good and discards the rest and is able to permanently maintain and continuously enhance its strengths through self-improvement and development.

Socialism with Chinese characteristics is a national system which guarantees the ownership of the people. China is a socialist country led by the working class and governed by the people's democratic dictatorship based on the alliance of workers and peasants, and all the power of the state belongs to the people. Socialism with Chinese characteristics upholds the organic unity of the leadership of the party, the ownership of the people and the rule of law, takes the leadership of the party as the fundamental guarantee of the ownership of the people and the rule of law, takes the ownership of the people as the essential characteristic of socialist democratic politics, takes the rule of law as the basic way for the party to lead the people to govern the country, and promotes the unification of these three approaches in the great implementation of socialist democratic politics in China. Comrade Xi Jinping stressed that: "Democracy is not an ornament and is not to be used as a mere decoration, but it is to be used on behalf of the people for solving problems requiring a solution." The system of the ownership of the people in China is concretely and realistically reflected in the rule of the CPC and state governance, in all aspects and at all levels of work of the party and state organs, in the implementation by the people, through various channels and forms and in accordance with the law, of the management of state affairs, economic and cultural undertakings, and the management of social affairs. It is a system which serves, and protects the fundamental rights and interests of, the entire population, rather than being one which serves the interests of one particular class or one specific group. This is the fundamental difference between socialism with Chinese characteristics and the capitalist system, and it is also the basis for the effective operation, continuous improvement and consolidation of the development of socialism with Chinese characteristics.

Socialism with Chinese characteristics is a national system which liberates and develops social productivity and enhances social vitality. Since the founding of new China, and especially since the implementation of reform and opening up, the successes in development and governance achieved by the CPC under the leadership of the Chinese people have attracted global attention. From a state of impoverishment to having the second largest economy in the world, from a situation whereby the people lacked adequate food and clothing to joining the ranks of the world's middle-income countries, from experiencing a shortage of goods to becoming the great power in global trade, from a state of being closed or semi-closed to the outside world to participating in global governance, from the periphery of the world system to moving increasingly closer to the centre of the world stage, China has experienced dramatic changes and passed through a period of industrialisation within decades through which it took developed countries hundreds of years to pass. China's miraculous rapid economic development and long-term social stability is fundamentally a miracle brought about by socialism with Chinese characteristics. The strong vitality and great superiority of socialism with

Chinese characteristics come together at one point, namely that this system is able to continuously promote the progress and development of a large country with a population of nearly 1.4 billion people, and ensure that the Chinese nation, with a history of more than five thousand years of civilisation, achieves the goal of the "Two Centenaries" and thus achieves great rejuvenation.

SOCIALISM WITH CHINESE CHARACTERISTICS KEEPS PACE WITH THE TIMES, AND IS CONSTANTLY IMPROVING AND DEVELOPING

Engels once said: "The so-called 'socialist society' is not anything immutable. Like all other social formations, it should be conceived in a state of constant flux and change". In connection with this, particularly in China, a semi-colonial and semi-feudal East Asian power which is economically and culturally backward, seizing national power and establishing a socialist system is a brand-new topic in the history of the development of Marxism, and it is even more vital to integrate the basic principles of Marxism with China's concrete reality, constantly explore practice and reform and innovate. Practice has proven that socialism with Chinese characteristics is a system that keeps pace with the times and continuously achieves self-improvement and development in the process of reform and opening up.

Socialism with Chinese characteristics is a good system with distinctive features and a high level of efficiency, but it is not yet a mature, complete, and perfect system. In view of the requirements of China's economic and social development and the expectations of the people, the new situation whereby the modern world is undergoing great changes unprecedented in the entirety of the past century, and the enormous challenge of achieving the great goal of China's long-term stability, there are still many aspects of China's national system and national system of governance requiring improvement and there is still a great mountain to climb for socialism with Chinese characteristics to attain to a state of greater maturity and completeness. In the new era, it is vital to adapt to the overall process of national modernisation, improve the level of scientific and democratic governance and rule according to the law, enhance the ability of state institutions to perform their duties and the ability of the people to manage state, economic, social, cultural and personal affairs in accordance with the law, achieve the institutionalisation, standardisation and proceduralisation of the governance of the party, the state and social affairs, and continuously improve the party's ability to govern the country effectively using socialism with Chinese characteristics.

The Fourth Plenary Session of the 19th CPC Central Committee focused on the important political issue of clarifying which systems and principles should be adhered to and consolidated, and what areas should be perfected and developed with regards to China's national system and national system of governance. The plenary session clarified the fundamental points to which the various institutions must adhere and the appropriate direction in which to perfect development, as well as laying out work which must be done. The plenary session not only expounded the major systems and principles that must be firmly adhered to, but also laid out the major reforms of institutional mechanisms that need to be deepened and the key tasks that need to be promoted. The plenary session thereby embodied the scientific methodology of correct innovation, the characteristics of systems integration, collaboration and efficiency, and also a strong problem-oriented approach. In doing so it pointed out the direction in which efforts should proceed for adhering to and improving socialism with Chinese characteristics in the new era and promoting the modernisation of the national system of governance and governability. It also provided standards for general compliance to stimulate greater institutional maturity and perfection. In the new era adherence to, and perfection of, socialism with Chinese characteristics, and the promotion of the modernisation of the national system of governance and governability have a more defined direction, position and set of guiding principles.

At the plenary session, Comrade Xi Jinping stressed that: "The reason why we are comprehensively deepening reform is not because socialism with Chinese characteristics is bad, but in order to make it even better. When we talk of consolidating confidence in institutions, this does not mean getting stuck in outdated ways, but rather to continue to eliminate systemic problems present in institutional mechanisms in order that China's institutions mature and endure." Comrade Xi Jinping also pointed out that: "Promoting the modernisation of the national system of governance and governability by no means equates to Westernisation or the adoption of capitalism."

China is a great power, and when it comes to the fundamental issue of the national system when faced with the major issues pertaining to the direction of development, will absolutely not speak out contradictory views, act secretively, or make subversive mistakes. Under the premise of adhering to and consolidating the fundamental, basic, and important institutions which have already been established and tested by practice, the party must persist with ideological emancipation, advancing with the times, and seeking truth from facts and pragmatism. Taking, upholding and perfecting socialism with

Chinese characteristics and promoting the modernisation of the national system of governance and governability as the principle axis, the party must deeply grasp China's developmental requirements and the trends of the times, resolutely breaking down all the ills of anachronistic ideology and systemic problems in institutional mechanisms, and continuing to deepen the reform of various institutional mechanisms in various sectors. The party must also deeply grasp laws regarding institutional construction, emphasise systemic, holistic and synergistic reforms, be adept at summing up practical experience and grassroots creativity, and act in a timely manner to ensure the accomplishment of results in theoretical and practical innovations at the institutional level, so that the superiority of socialism with Chinese characteristics will continue to be strengthened and fully manifested.

(Originally published in the *People's Daily* on 26 December 2019)

CHAPTER TWO

THE NEW DEVELOPMENT OF MARXIST STATE DOCTRINE – THE 'NINE FIRSTS' OF THE FOURTH PLENARY SESSION OF THE 19TH CPC COMMITTEE

The *Decision of the CPC Central Committee on Several Major Issues Regarding Upholding and Perfecting Socialism with Chinese Characteristics and Promoting the Modernisation of the National System of Governance and Governability*, which was considered and adopted by the Fourth Plenary Session of the 19th CPC Central Committee (hereinafter referred to as the *Decision*), is an iconic achievement of contemporary Chinese Marxist national doctrine, and a political declaration aimed at raising the banner of the national system and the construction of the national system of governance in the new era. It not only contains many new theoretical generalisations, but also many new practical initiatives. The plenary session and the *Decision* gave rise to a number of 'firsts', predominantly characterised by the following nine major aspects.

Adhering to and perfecting socialism with Chinese characteristics and promoting the modernisation of the national system of governance and governability are major issues related to the prosperity of the party and national affairs, China's long-term stability, and peace and prosperity of the people. It also constitutes the major task of achieving the goal of the "Two Centenaries", the fundamental requirement for advancing reform and opening up in the new era, and also a powerful guarantee for addressing risks and challenges and gaining the initiative in various areas. The Fourth Plenary Session of the 19th CPC Central Committee marked the first time in the history of the CPC that a plenary session had been devoted to study and making arrangements to address this major issue. This constituted a comprehensive political, wide-ranging, and strategic consideration of the CPC Central Committee with Comrade Xi Jinping as its core and was a major policy decision based on a present and long-term perspective which amply embodied the historic role of strategic vision with acute foresight while striving for the prosperity of the nation.

Looking back on the whole process of socialism from its birth to the present time, taking over national administration in China, an economically and culturally backward East Asian power, there establishing socialist institutions and then building a modern socialist power, is an unprecedented new manifestation in the history of Marxist development. Similarly, establishing and perfecting a socialist national system and a national system of governance in China, a developing country with a long and profound history, extremely large territory and population, a highly complex ethnic structure and a very large-scale economy, constitutes an extremely difficult task which Marxist classic writers have never spoken about, and there are no readily available models from past socialist practice anywhere in the world from which to learn. However, the CPC rose to the challenge, persisted in integrating the basic principles of Marxism with China's concrete reality, continuously explored practice, reformed and innovated, established and perfected a socialist system, formed and developed the party's leadership and economic, political, cultural, social, eco-civilisation-related, military, diplomatic and other institutions, strengthened and improved national governance, and made historic achievements. In particular, after the 18th CPC National Congress, the CPC Central Committee, with Comrade Xi Jinping as its core, has led the whole party and the people to uphold and refine socialism with Chinese characteristics, and to advance the modernisation of the national system of governance and governability in order to achieve significant theoretical, practical and institutional achievements. These achievements of China's socialist system constitute a great innovation in the history of human institutions and are truly remarkable.

The Fourth Plenary Session of the 19th CPC Central Committee comprehensively summarised the achievements made, experience accumulated, and principles formed in the construction of China's national system and national governance through the party's leading of the people in the practice of exploring socialism with Chinese characteristics. The plenary session systematically expounded on the significance, general requirements, scientific connotations and practical approaches of upholding and perfecting socialism with Chinese characteristics, and of promoting the modernisation of the national system of governance and governability. This constitutes the latest major achievement of Xi Jinping's thought on socialism with Chinese characteristics for a new era. This major achievement, which scientifically answers the fundamental question regarding the kind of socialism with Chinese characteristics that should be upheld and developed in the new era in terms of institutional form, and also clarifies how this should be achieved, is a great historical contribution of the CPC to Marxism and scientific socialism.

Marxism tells us that the proletariat cannot simply use existing state machinery to achieve its own ends after seizing power, but rather that it is necessary to establish political institutions based on the dictatorship of the proletariat to replace the state machinery of the ruling class. Socialism with Chinese characteristics and the national system of governance constitute an entirely new national system and national system of governance established through the creative application of the Marxist doctrine of the state through continuous exploration and practice, which guarantees the ownership of the people for several hundred million people. It was established by the party after it united and led the people of China to overthrow the reactionary rule of imperialism, feudalism and bureaucratic capitalism.

The formation and development of socialism with Chinese characteristics and the national system of governance drew on the valuable experience of the CPC in ruling in the base areas during the period in which it led the New Democratic Revolution and underwent three major historical stages of development 29 years after the founding of new China, 34 years after the Third Plenary Session of the 11th Central Committee of the Party, and seven years since the 18th CPC National Congress. The formation and development of socialism with Chinese characteristics and the national system of governance have been the substance of the party and the people's long-term struggle from one generation to the next, achieved by passing through untold hardships and at great cost.

The *Decision* produced for the first time the new summary: "Socialism with Chinese characteristics is a scientific system formed by the party and the people through a long-term process of practical exploration", which constitutes a scientific summary of the course of the formation of China's national system and the national system of governance. General Secretary Xi Jinping emphasised that the national system of governance is a system for managing the country under the leadership of the party, and national governability is the capacity to employ the national system to manage all aspects of social affairs. The *Decision* further makes it clear that all the work and activities of China's national governance are carried out in accordance with socialism with Chinese characteristics, and that China's national system of governance and governability constitute the concentrated embodiment of socialism with Chinese characteristics and the capacity to implement it. This statement expounds for the first time the intrinsic relationship between socialism with Chinese characteristics and the national system of governance and governability and has major theoretical and practical significance.

The national system is the fundamental basis and core of national governance, and all the work and activities of national governance are carried out in accordance with the national system. The system undoubtedly plays a fundamental, overall, and long-term role in national governance. However, without effective governability, it is difficult for good institutions and governance systems to function. Although the national system and the national system of governance are closely related to national governability, they are not the same thing. It also cannot be said that the more mature the national system, the more perfect the national system of governance will be and thereby national governability will automatically be stronger. Therefore, the *Decision* clearly proposed improving governability as a major task in the building up of cadres in the new era, and, through strengthening ideological refinement, political experience, practical exercise and professional training, propelling the masses of cadres to perform their duties, exercise power, and carry out their work in strict accordance with the system, thereby advancing the promotion of the capacity for, and level of, work in all areas, including the overall composition of the "Five-Pronged Approach" and the strategic composition of the "Four Comprehensives".

Only by earnestly implementing the requirements of the *Decision*, striving to improve the comprehensive quality of cadres at all levels and managers in all fields, and striving to improve the management capabilities and working ability of party and state organs, enterprises and institutions, and people's organisations, can the governability of the whole country be greatly improved, can the national system of governance operate more effectively, and can the strengths of China's system be better translated into more effective national governance.

THE FIRST TIME THAT THE SIGNIFICANT STRENGTHS OF CHINA'S NATIONAL SYSTEM AND NATIONAL SYSTEM OF GOVERNANCE WERE SUMMARISED IN 13 ASPECTS

Institutional strength is a country's greatest strength, and institutional competition is the most fundamental manifestation of competition between countries. If the institutions are stable and strong, then so is the country. The most fundamental reason why the Chinese nation has managed, in the 70 years since the founding of new China, to usher in a great leap from standing up and getting rich to becoming strong, is because the party has led the people to establish and perfect socialism with Chinese characteristics, constantly strengthening and improving national governance, such that China's national system and the national system of governance have gained more and more comparative advantages in the context of international competition and displayed great vitality. The *Decision* systematically summarises the 13 significant strengths of China's national system and national system of governance, and scientifically reveals the institutional reasons for new China's developmental achievements over the past 70 years and supports the enhancement of the confidence of the whole party and all the peoples of China, leading the multi-faceted strengths of China's national system

19

and national system of governance to be more fully exhibited.

There are no two identical political systems in the world, and it is not possible for the political systems of individual countries to rely on a single authority to determine what is the correct approach. Socialism with Chinese characteristics and China's national system of governance grew from the soil of Chinese society, were formed by the long-term practice of revolution, construction and reform, and are enriched by being rooted in the profound historical and cultural traditions accumulated by the more than 5000 years of Chinese civilisation and beneficial achievements absorbed and learnt from human institutional civilisation. This is all centrally reflected in the characteristics and strengths of socialism with Chinese characteristics.

In a speech at the 60th anniversary of the Founding of the National People's Congress in 2014, General Secretary Xi Jinping insightfully stated:

"[The criteria required] for evaluating whether or not a country's political system is democratic and effective are mainly whether or not the leadership of the country can transition in an orderly manner in accordance with the law, whether or not the people can manage state and social affairs and economic and cultural undertakings in accordance with the law, whether or not the people can freely express their interests, whether or not all sections of society can participate effectively in the political life of the country, whether or not national decision-making can be achieved scientifically and democratically, whether or not all kinds of talented individuals can enter the national leadership and management systems by way of fair competition, whether or not the ruling party can achieve leadership in state affairs in accordance with the provisions of the Constitution, and whether or not effective control and supervision can be implemented in the exercising of authority."

The 13 significant strengths outlined in the *Decision* are the scientific conclusions reached by examining the practice of socialism with Chinese characteristics using the "Eight Whethers". It is therein proven that China's national system and national system of governance constitute a set of practicable, truly efficacious and efficient institutions and governance systems which have not only ensured that China has produced a miracle of rapid economic development of a kind rarely seen and the miracle of long-term social stability, but also provided a new option in terms of routes to modernisation for developing countries, and contributed China's wisdom and Chinese programs to mankind in its search for how to build better social institutions.

The reason why China's national system and national system of governance have many significant strengths lies in the CPC's insistence on integrating the basic principles of Marxism with China's concrete reality, unifying the pioneering of the correct road, developing innovative theory and building effective institutions, so that China's national system and national system of governance not only embody the basic principles of scientific socialism, but also possess distinctly Chinese characteristics, national characteristics and characteristics representative of the times. It is also because China's national system and national system of governance have always represented the fundamental interests of the vast majority of the people, ensured that the people are the masters of the country, reflected the common will of the people, and safeguarded the legitimate rights of the people, thereby winning the support of the Chinese people. It also lies in the fact that China's national system and national system of governance have never excluded the governance experience of any other country which is conducive to China's development and progress, but upholds a China-centred approach, keeps what is good and discards the rest, and is able to permanently maintain and continuously enhance its remarkable superiority and great vitality through self-improvement and development.

Institutions are the foundation of national governance, peace and stability. In 1980, Comrade Deng Xiaoping summed up the lessons of the Cultural Revolution by stating that: "The problems of leadership and organisational institutions are more fundamental, global, stable and long-term", and: "If institutions are good, they can prevent bad people from running amok, but if institutions are bad then they can prevent the good people from being able to do their work well and can even create a contrary effect."

The 12th CPC National Congress clearly put forward the general policy of China following its own unique path and building socialism with Chinese characteristics, and also made arrangements for improving the party's practice of democratic centralism, reforming the leadership structure and the cadre system, and conducting party rectification in a systematic and planned fashion.

The 13th CPC National Congress expounded and made arrangements for the reform of China's political system. The

14th CPC National Congress determined that the goal of China's economic restructuring would be to establish a socialist market economy, clearly proposing the provisional establishment of a new economic system in the 1990s, in order to form a more mature and more finalised system in all aspects by the 100th anniversary of the founding of the CPC. The 15th, 16th and 17th CPC National Congresses all put forward clear requirements for institutional construction.

Since the 18th CPC National Congress, the CPC Central Committee, with Comrade Xi Jinping as its core, has taken a strong historical role in putting institutional construction in a more prominent position, taking the opportunity to deepen reform in important areas, resolutely eliminating all the shortcomings in ideology and institutional mechanisms that hinder scientific development, and striving to build institutions which are complete, adhere to scientific standards, and operate effectively. The Third Plenary Session of the 18th CPC Central Committee established improving and developing socialism with Chinese characteristics, and promoting the modernisation of the national system of governance and governability, as the overall objectives of the comprehensive deepening of reform, and to that end launched 336 major reform initiatives. After nearly six years of efforts, the reform of important areas and key links achieved remarkable results, and basic institutions and systems in major areas had been basically formed.

It was on the basis of these practical achievements that the *Decision* systematically summarised and set out the overall objectives of adhering to and perfecting socialism with Chinese characteristics, and the promotion of the modernisation of the national system of governance and governability. These overall objectives further clarified the strategic objectives of the "Three-step Development Strategy" which the party had already benchmarked, namely, to establish a moderately prosperous society by the 100th anniversary of the establishment of the CPC, to basically achieve socialist modernisation by 2035, and to build China into a prosperous, powerful, democratic, civilised, harmonious and beautiful modern socialist power by the 100th anniversary of the founding of new China. Specifically, by the 100th anniversary of the establishment of the CPC, all institutions should achieve remarkable results through becoming more mature and finalised; by 2035, all institutions should be further improved and the national system of governance and governability are to have been basically modernised; by the 100th anniversary of the founding of new China, the modernisation of the national system of governance and governability are to have been fully achieved, such that socialism with Chinese characteristics will be more consolidated and its superiority fully demonstrated. This is the first time in the party's major documents that it has focused on individually advancing the overall objectives of the "Three-step Development Strategy" in the modernisation of the national system of governance and governability, and fully reflected the historical orientation of socialism with Chinese characteristics in the new era of the CPC Central Committee, with Comrade Xi Jinping as its core, making strategic arrangements to adhere to and improve socialism with Chinese characteristics and to promote the modernisation of the national system of governance and governability.

THE FIRST TIME THAT THE INSTITUTIONS PLAYING THE
FUNDAMENTAL STRUCTURAL ROLE OF "FOUR BEAMS AND EIGHT
PILLARS" WITHIN SOCIALISM WITH CHINESE CHARACTERISTICS
WERE CLEARLY DEFINED AS THE FUNDAMENTAL INSTITUTIONS,
THE BASIC INSTITUTIONS AND THE MAJOR INSTITUTIONS

Socialism with Chinese characteristics constitutes a great historical creation of the CPC since reform and opening up in leading the people of China into the Sinicisation of Marxism. This creation, in the practical aspect, opened the way for socialism with Chinese characteristics, and in the theoretical aspect shaped the theoretical system of socialism with Chinese characteristics comprised of Deng Xiaoping Theory, the important concept of the "Three Represents", a scientific outlook on development, and Xi Jinping Thought on Socialism with Chinese Characteristics for a New Era. In the institutional aspect, it established socialism with Chinese characteristics, and in the cultural aspect, it upheld and developed the culture of socialism with Chinese characteristics.

Three major CPC documents have scientifically expounded on several aspects of socialism with Chinese characteristics. In his speech at the meeting to commemorate the 90th anniversary of the founding of the CPC and the report of the 18th CPC National Congress, Comrade Hu Jintao explained the scientific connotation of the path of socialism with Chinese characteristics, the theoretical system of socialism with Chinese characteristics, and the scientific essence of socialism with Chinese characteristics. He also clearly advanced the idea that socialism with Chinese characteristics is a complete set of interrelated and interconnected systems formed in various fields such as economics, politics, culture and society, and cited the fundamental institutions, the basic political institutions, the basic economic institutions and the various specific institutions in each field based on these.

General Secretary Xi Jinping clearly advanced the important concepts of the "culture of socialism with Chinese characteristics" and "cultural confidence" in his report at the 19th CPC National Congress, and individually and scientifically situated the historical role of the path of socialism with Chinese characteristics, the theoretical system of socialism with Chinese characteristics, and the culture of socialism with Chinese characteristics. Xi stressed that the party should more consciously strengthen confidence in the path, theory, institutions and culture which the party upholds, and expanded and fleshed out the scientific meaning of socialism with Chinese characteristics in the new era.

The valuable contribution of the *Decision* lies in the fact that, for the first time, the basic components of socialism with Chinese characteristics and the national system of governance were systematically summarised from 13 aspects, and the institutions playing the fundamental structural role of "Four Beams and Eight Pillars" within socialism with Chinese characteristics were clearly defined as the fundamental institutions, the basic institutions and the major institutions.

The fundamental institutions refer to those institutions that reflect the essential nature and fundamental characteristics of socialism with Chinese characteristics and embody the prescriptiveness of socialism with Chinese characteristics; these institutions constitute the fundamental basis of statehood. Examples of these institutions include the system of party leadership, the institution of the NPC, the fundamental institutions upholding the guiding position of Marxism in the realm of ideology, and the party's absolute leadership of the PLA.

The basic institutions refer to those institutions that embody China's socialist nature, determine China's basic form, and regulate China's political and economic relations. Examples of these institutions include those enabling multi-party cooperation and political consultation under the leadership of the CPC, the system of regional ethnic autonomy, the system of grassroots mass autonomy, the basic socialist economic system and so on.

The major institutions refer to the subjective institutions in all aspects of national governance derived from the fundamental and the basic institutions, including economic, political, cultural, social, eco-civilisation-related, military, diplomatic and other institutions. This clear exposition furnished by the *Decision* constitutes an important institutional arrangement for all aspects of party and national undertakings, representing a more systematic, holistic and standardised national system and national system of governance.

THE FIRST TIME THAT THE LEADING POSITION OF THE SYSTEM OF PARTY LEADERSHIP WITHIN CHINA'S NATIONAL SYSTEM AND NATIONAL SYSTEM OF GOVERNANCE WAS SPECIFIED

Promoting the modernisation of the national system and the national system of governance is a process of advancing with the times, and likewise the party's understanding of this issue is also advancing with the times. In the past when talking of the implications of socialism with Chinese characteristics, the focus would generally be on economics, politics, culture, society, eco-civilisation, military affairs, diplomacy, and party construction, and this was clearly the correct approach.

Since the 18th CPC National Congress, General Secretary Xi Jinping has made the clear and significant assertion that: "The most essential characteristic of socialism with Chinese characteristics is the leadership of the CPC; the greatest strength of socialism with Chinese characteristics is the leadership of the CPC; and the party is the supreme force in political leadership", which has served to deepen understanding of the CPC's law of governance by way of a new perspective.

From a practical point of view, the CPC Central Committee has comprehensively strengthened and improved the leadership of the party, continuously improved its institutional mechanisms, formed a set of institutional norms and working mechanisms which uphold it, and transformed it into a superior institution for national governance. This has enabled socialism with Chinese characteristics to manifest greater dynamism and vitality. Practice has amply proven that this system of party leadership is China's fundamental leadership institution, and it is undoubtedly the indispensable and fundamental institution taking the role of coordination, leadership and directorship for socialism with Chinese characteristics in the context of the national system and the national system of governance.

The *Decision* put forward the important concept of "the system of party leadership", prioritises the important concept of upholding and perfecting the system of party leadership, and improving the scientific, democratic and legal governance of the party within the process of upholding and improving socialism with Chinese characteristics, promoting the modernisation of the national system of governance and governability. It also highlighted the leading position of the system of party leadership in the national system and national system of governance, and expounded for the first time the basic elements of upholding and perfecting the system of party leadership from six aspects, from the guiding ideology to major viewpoints to concrete measures, which all embody the requirements of upholding and strengthening the leadership of the party and achieving the "Two Upholds". These new summaries and provisions captured the key and fundamental aspects of the construction of the national system and national governance, and are conducive to institutionalising, concretising and standardising the party's leadership, ensuring that the leadership of the party is exercised in all aspects and sectors of national governance.

The basic socialist economic system amongst all economic systems is characterised by its long-term and stable nature and has a decisive influence on the attributes and mode of economic development of an economy. The *Decision* clearly advances the simultaneous development of a multi-ownership economy with public ownership as the main feature, the coexistence of various methods of distribution with distribution according to work as the main feature, and the socialist market economy and other basic socialist economic institutions. It not only reflects the superiority of the socialist system but is also compatible with the level of development of social productivity in the primary stage of socialism in China and constitutes a great creation of the party and the people. This statement, which for the first time incorporated the mode of distribution and the socialist market economy into the scope of the basic economic system, constitutes a major theoretical innovation by the CPC.

A society's basic economic system is determined by the relationship between that society's productivity and its production, mainly made up of three basic components: ownership of social means of production, means of social distribution and allocation of social resources. Since reform and opening up the CPC has profoundly captured and analysed positive and negative [economic] experiences both from China and from overseas, and, starting from China's basic national conditions in the context of the primary stage of socialism, has emancipated the mind and sought truth from facts. It has also achieved the transformation from a single public ownership economy to a multi-ownership economy with public ownership as the main feature, the transformation from a single mode of distribution according to work to the coexistence of various methods of distribution with distribution according to work as the main feature, and the transformation from a highly centralised planned economy to a socialist market economy, thereby greatly liberating and developing social productivity, giving rise to the miracle of rapid economic development.

On the basis of practical exploration and practical tests, the Third Plenary Session of the 12th CPC Central Committee clearly stated that the socialist economy is a planned commodity economy based on public ownership. Then, the Third Plenary Session of the 14th CPC Central Committee further proposed that it is necessary to adhere to the common development of multiple economic components with public ownership as the main feature.

Then, the 15th CPC National Congress clearly proposed for the first time that: "the common development of a multi-ownership economy mainly characterised by public ownership is a basic economic system in the primary stage of socialism in China", marking the formal establishment of China's socialist basic economic system.

The 16th CPC National Congress went on to clearly put forward the important idea of the "Two Unwaverings", namely unwaveringly consolidating and developing the public ownership economy, and unwaveringly encouraging, supporting and guiding the development of the non-public ownership economy.

The Third Plenary Session of the 18th CPC Central Committee then clearly stated that both the public and non-public economies are important components of the socialist market economy and constitute important foundations for China's economic and social development. All these and other advances demonstrate the party's constantly deepening understanding of the socialist basic economic system.

One of the major innovations of the Fourth Plenary Session of the 19th CPC Central Committee was to provide a new overview of the socialist basic economic system, establishing the coexistence of various distribution modes with distribution according to work as the main feature, and the rise of the socialist market economic system, as the basic economic system. This constituted a scientific summary of China's experience of reform and opening up over a period of more than 40 years, especially of new experiences since the 18th CPC National Congress and provided theoretical and institutional support for promoting high-quality economic development and building a modern economic system.

The *Decision* stated: "Upholding the fundamental system of Marxism being in the guiding position in the field of ideology". This was the first time in the important party documents that the guiding position of Marxism in the field of ideology was defined as a fundamental system of the party and the state.

The birth of Marxism constitutes the greatest and most important event in the history of human thought and has led to unprecedented historical changes in human society. Marx and Engels pointed out in *The German Ideology* that: "The ideas of the ruling class are in every epoch the ruling ideas, ie the class which is the ruling material force of society, is at the same time its ruling intellectual force." The history of human social development demonstrates that every country and society has a dominant ideology, as is the case in socialist countries and societies, as well as in capitalist countries and societies. The CPC is a political party having Marxism as its banner, and all the achievements of Chinese revolution, construction and reform have been accomplished under the guidance of Marxism and the Sinicisation of Marxism, thus determining that the guiding ideology in the field of ideology in China must be Marxism.

Today's world is undergoing great changes not seen in a hundred years, and China is in a critical period for achieving the great rejuvenation of the Chinese nation, facing both historical opportunities with great potential and also unprecedented risks and challenges. In the face of the complex situation of increasing diversity of social ideologies, increasingly diverse social values and an influx of ideas in the ideological field, it is crucial to unswervingly uphold and consolidate the guiding position of Marxism in the field of ideology and promote the ideological unity of all the people of China. Only then will it be possible to overcome all kinds of difficulties and obstacles along the way and win new victories in the new era.

In a major speech at the Third Plenary Session of the 18th CPC Central Committee, General Secretary Xi Jinping said:

"Ideological work is one of the party's extremely important works. Facing the complex situation of reform, development, and stability, along with profound changes in the diversity of social ideologies and the media landscape, at the same times as concentrating on economic construction we must not relax or weaken our ideological work even for a moment. We must hold the leadership, management and discourse power of ideological work firmly in our hands, and never let go; otherwise, we will make irreparable historical mistakes."

The *Decision* clearly defines upholding the guiding position of Marxism in the field of ideology as a fundamental system of the party and the state, and it constitutes a major initiative to firmly grasp the leadership, management and discourse power of ideological work at the level of national system and national governance. This reflects the great importance that the CPC Central Committee, with Comrade Xi Jinping as its core, attaches to ideological work and ideological security in the new era.

THE FIRST TIME THAT THE IMPORTANT POSITION OF
THE PARTY AND STATE SUPERVISORY SYSTEM WITHIN THE
SYSTEM OF SOCIALISM WITH CHINESE CHARACTERISTICS
AND NATIONAL GOVERNANCE WAS DEFINED

The party and state supervisory system constitutes an important institutional guarantee enabling the party to achieve self-purification, self-improvement, self-innovation and self-development within the context of long-term governance. The *Decision*, in clearly stating 13 important tasks pertaining to upholding and perfecting socialism with Chinese characteristics and promoting the modernisation of the national system of governance and governability, established "adhering to and perfecting the party and state supervisory system, strengthening the control and monitoring of mechanisms for the exercise of power" as one distinct aspect within the list and made institutional arrangements for this. This is the first time this was established in important party documents, marking the attainment by the party within the context of long-term governance of a new level of understanding of self-revolution, permanence on the cutting edge, and political purity.

How to extricate China from a historical cycle characterised by the Confucian saying of "a country falls as abruptly and rapidly as it rises" is a major theoretical and practical problem that the CPC has been constantly exploring. Within the context of the overall leadership and long-term governance of the party, it is necessary for the party to improve its self-supervision and strengthen its supervision of state organs in order to constantly enhance its capacity for self-purification, ensure the integrity of cadres, clean government and political sobriety.

Since the 18th CPC National Congress, the CPC Central Committee with Comrade Xi Jinping as its core has focused on the long-term stability of the party and the state, promoted the reform of supervisory institutions from a political and comprehensive perspective, and preliminarily formed the overall framework of the party and state supervisory system.

The 19th CPC National Congress profoundly summarised the CPC's experience of comprehensive and strict party governance since the 18th CPC National Congress, and clearly advanced the strategic task of "building a unified command, comprehensive coverage, and an authoritative and efficient supervisory system for the party." The Second Plenary Session of the 19th CPC Central Committee deliberated and adopted the *Recommendations of the CPC Central Committee on Amending Some Parts of the Constitution*. On the basis of the proposal, the constitutional amendments deliberated and adopted at the first session of the 13th National People's Congress specifically added the Supervisory Commission, establishing the legal status of the Commission as a state institution. This constituted a major adjustment to China's political system, political power and political relations, a state supervision system executed at the highest level and in comprehensive fashion, and the enrichment and perfection of the supervisory system of socialism with Chinese characteristics.

Since the 19th CPC National Congress, under the strong leadership of the CPC Central Committee, major results have been achieved in the promotion of the reform of the party's system of discipline inspection, the reform of the state supervisory system and the reform of the discipline inspection and supervisory institutions. The supervisory committees and discipline committees at all levels work together to achieve the unity of intra-party supervision and state supervision through daily supervision, supervision of dispatched personnel and inspection supervision, and promote the routinisation and normalisation of supervision and inspection, making the institutions of party and state supervision more complete, scientific and orderly. All these have provided powerful institutions and legal protection for the consolidation and development of the achievements of the party's comprehensive and strict governance since the 18th CPC National Congress and laid a solid foundation for the establishment of a centralised, unified, authoritative and efficient system of party and state supervision.

Perfecting the party and state supervisory system is a difficult and complex systematic project. The *Decision* aimed to enhance the severity, synergy and effectiveness of supervision, form a power operation mechanism which is scientific in its decision-making, resolute in its implementation and powerful in its supervisory activities, in order to ensure that the power bestowed by the party and the people is always used for the well-being of the people and to achieve the full coverage of supervision of all officials exercising public power. It advanced clear, highly targeted and operational requirements and initiatives from the three aspects of perfecting the system of party and state supervision, perfecting the mechanisms for the allocation and restriction of power operations, and building an integrated institutional mechanism which deters, disenables, and discourages corruption.

In addition to the "The Nine Firsts" outlined above, the *Decision*, on the basis of summing up practical experience, further elaborated on the system of the ownership of the people, the socialist system of laws with Chinese characteristics, socialist administrative institutions with Chinese characteristics, institutions for the prosperity and development of advanced socialist culture, integrated institutions for the safeguarding of livelihood in urban and rural areas, institutions of social governance for shared construction and governance, institutions of eco-civilisation, the absolute leadership system of the party over the PLA, and the system of "One Country, Two Systems", etc. The *Decision* also put forward a series of innovative theoretical perspectives and major reform measures.

In summary, the Fourth Plenary Session of the 19th CPC Central Committee and the *Decision* comprehensively answered the major political question of what China's national system and national system of governance should uphold and consolidate, and what they should perfect and develop. The series of new ideas, perspectives and measures they advanced in connection with the new development of Marxist national doctrine are certain to be recorded in the annals of the CPC.

(Originally published in the *Study Times* on 18 November 2019)

CHAPTER THREE

A GREAT INNOVATION IN THE HISTORY OF HUMAN INSTITUTIONS AND CIVILISATION

Editor's commentary: The *Decision of the CPC Central Committee on Several Major Issues Regarding Adhering to and Perfecting Socialism with Chinese Characteristics and Promoting the Modernisation of the National System of Governance and Governability* deliberated and adopted by the Fourth Plenary Session of the 19th CPC Central Committee, accurately grasped the evolutionary direction and law of China's national system and national system of governance, taking into account the overall and long-term development of the party and the state, and profoundly answered the important political question of "what to uphold and consolidate, and what to perfect and develop". It thereby expounded on the important institutions and principles that must be firmly upheld, and also made arrangements for major tasks and initiatives for promoting institutional construction. But how is the spirit of the Fourth Plenary Session of the CPC 19th Central Committee to be correctly understood, and how is the spirit of the plenary session to be grasped and implemented? This publication launched a series of reports in the "authoritative interview" column, interviewing delegates, comrades in charge of the relevant ministries and comrades in the document-drafting group, in order to interpret the spirit of the plenary session.

The Fourth Plenary Session of the 19th CPC Central Committee made comprehensive arrangements to uphold and improve socialism with Chinese characteristics and promote the modernisation of the national system of governance and governability. Recently, our reporter conducted an exclusive interview with He Yiting, deputy director in charge of the daily work of the CPC Central Party School (China National School of Administration) and asked him to interpret the spirit of the Fourth Plenary Session of the 19th CPC Central Committee.

Reporter: Please could you talk about the historical stages passed through during the formation and development of socialism with Chinese characteristics and the national system of governance.

He Yiting: Socialism with Chinese characteristics and the national system of governance constitute a new national system and system of governance established by the CPC after the CPC united and led the people of China to overthrow the reactionary rule of imperialism, feudalism and bureaucratic capitalism. This system has made creative use of the Marxist state doctrine of China and profoundly summarised both positive and negative political experiences in China and overseas. It was established during continual exploration of practice, and constant reform and innovation, and ensures the ownership of the people for China's vast population. This constitutes a great innovation in the history of human institutions and civilisation.

The formation and development of socialism with Chinese characteristics and the national system of governance, drawing on the valuable experience of the CPC in ruling in the base areas during the period of leading the New Democratic Revolution, has gone through three major historical stages during the 70 years of new China.

Between the founding of new China and the Third Plenary Session of the 11th CPC Central Committee, the party established the national system of the ownership of the people, established the basic socialist system, explored a path of socialist construction suited to China's national conditions, and established the fundamental political preconditions and institutional foundations for the entirety of development and progress in contemporary China.

Between the Third Plenary Session of the 11th CPC Central Committee and the 18th CPC National Congress, the party clearly advanced following China's own path and building socialism with Chinese characteristics, actively promoted the reform of economic and other institutions, established socialism with Chinese characteristics, constantly improved national governance, and provided a solid institutional guarantee for reform, opening up and modernisation.

Since the 18th CPC National Congress, by comprehensively promoting the general layout of the "Five-Pronged Approach" and coordinating the promotion of the strategic layout of the "Four Comprehensives", the party has promoted the betterment of socialism with Chinese characteristics, a significant improvement in the level of modernisation of the national system of governance and governability, and provided a strong guarantee for the historic transformation and historic achievements of the party and the national cause.

Reporter: Since the 18th CPC National Congress, what historic achievements has the party made in promoting the construction of the national system and the national system of governance?

He Yiting: Since the 18th CPC National Congress, the CPC Central Committee, with Comrade Xi Jinping as its core, has taken on a strong historical role in putting institutional construction in a more prominent position and has seized the opportunity to deepen reform in important areas. The Third Plenary Session of the 18th CPC Central Committee set the overall goal of improving and developing socialism with Chinese characteristics, promoting the modernisation of the national system of governance and governability as the overall goal of deepening reform in an all-round way. The plenary session launched 336 major reform initiatives and upheld a combination of problem-oriented and goal-oriented approaches in the practice of the comprehensive deepening of reform that has followed, actively promoting the construction of the national system and the modernisation of the national system of governance and attaining to historic achievements.

The first goal was to uphold and improve the system of party leadership. In order to improve the system of safeguarding the authority of the CPC Central Committee and centralising and unifying leadership, the plenary session clearly proposed to spur on the party to strengthen the "Four Consciousnesses", uphold the "Four Matters of Confidence" and achieve the "Two Safeguards", and consciously maintain a high degree of consistency with the CPC Central Committee with Comrade Xi Jinping as its core, in ideology, politics and action. It also sought to reform and improve the leadership system of the CPC Central Committee as it pertains to major tasks, improve the system for reporting to the CPC Central Committee, facilitate the central role of the party's overall leadership and coordination of all parties, and continuously improve the party's ability to provide direction, make overall plans, set policies and promote reform.

The second goal was to uphold and improve the comprehensive intensification of the system of party governance. The CPC Central Committee advanced and implemented the general requirements of the party's construction and organisational line in the new era, and, taking the political construction of the party as the guide, implemented institutional construction throughout, and comprehensively promoted all aspects of the party's construction. The plenary session improved the system of party responsibility in an all-round way, strictly enforced the party's political discipline and rules, deepened the reform of the discipline inspection and supervisory system, set up a national monitoring committee, improved the party and state supervisory system, strengthened the control and monitoring of mechanisms for the exercise of power, achieved an overwhelming victory in the fight against corruption, demonstrated new developments in the political ecology of the party, and ensured the party became a strong core of leadership in forging revolution.

The third goal was to uphold and improve the socialist system of laws with Chinese characteristics. The *Decision of the CPC Central Committee on a Few Major Issues Regarding the Comprehensive Promotion of the Rule of Law* adopted by the Fourth Plenary Session of the 18th CPC Central Committee made comprehensive arrangements to build a socialist country ruled by law in the new era, and the construction of the rule of law, especially the reform of the judicial system, has been carried out with unprecedented intensity. Thus ,the rule of law has been comprehensively further advanced, the construction of the rule of law in China has made firm progress, the socialist system of laws with Chinese characteristics has been constantly improved, and the concept of the rule of law throughout the whole of society has been significantly enhanced. After the 19th CPC National Congress, the Law on Supervision, and the Law on National Medals and Honorary Titles were enacted, and significant new progress was made in legislative work.

The fourth goal was to uphold and improve the system of the ownership of the people. The CPC Central Committee organically unified the party leadership, the ownership of the people and the rule of law, and continuously strengthened the institutional guarantee of the ownership of the people. The plenary session upheld and improved the institution of the NPC, executed at the highest level and in comprehensive fashion, clearly put forward facilitating the leading role of the NPC and its Standing Committee in legislative work, set up special new social construction committees at all levels of the NPC, and optimised the Standing Committee of the NPC and the composition of the special committees. The CPC Central Committee issued and implemented a series of supporting documents, such as *Opinions on Strengthening Socialist Consultative Democracy*, to consolidate and develop the patriotic united front through coordinated promotion of consultation between political parties, consultations of the NPC, government consultations, consultations of the CPPCC, of people's organisations, at the grassroots level and of social organisations.

The fifth goal was to uphold and improve the socialist economic system with Chinese characteristics. The plenary session focused on the liberation and development of social productivity, the liberation and enhancement of social vitality, and constantly improving and developing the socialist basic economic system. It improved the socialist market economy to amply facilitate the decisive role of the market in the allocation of resources, and better facilitated the role of the government. As a result, the system of national macroeconomic management has been continuously improved and various market players have constantly stimulated vitality. The plenary session comprehensively implemented new developmental concepts, further promoted supply-side structural reform, accelerated innovative national construction, and implemented a strategy for rural revitalisation. It also persisted in promoting major strategies such as the construction of the "One Belt, One Road" initiative, synergistic development in the Beijing-Tianjin-Hebei region, the development of the Yangtze River Economic Belt, and the construction of the Guangdong, Hong Kong and Macao Bay Area. As a result, the new open economic system was gradually improved, and China's economic strength and comprehensive national strength have been significantly enhanced.

Since the 18th CPC National Congress, historic progress has also been made in upholding and perfecting institutions pertaining to culture, society, eco-civilisation, and military and foreign affairs. Socialism with Chinese characteristics has demonstrated full vitality in self-improvement and development, creating not only the globally acknowledged miracle of economic development, but also the miracle of long-term national political and social stability.

Reporter：Please could you talk about the new arrangements made by the Fourth Plenary Session of the 19th CPC Central Committee to promote socialism with Chinese characteristics and the construction of the national system of governance?

He Yiting：The Fourth Plenary Session of the 19th CPC Central Committee comprehensively answered the important political question of what our national system and national system of governance should "uphold and consolidate, perfect and develop", and made new and important arrangements to promote socialism with Chinese characteristics and the construction of the national system of governance in the new era.

The first thing it did was to further clarify the overall requirements and objectives of upholding and perfecting socialism with Chinese characteristics and promoting the modernisation of the national system of governance and governability. This overall requirement, in a nutshell, is to adhere to the party's basic theoretical guidance, the centralised and unified leadership of the party, the emancipation of the mind, seeking truth from facts, reform and innovation, and the correct path and methods. This overall objective, the strategic objective of the "Three-step Development Strategy", namely, the targets already established by the party to build a moderately prosperous society by the 100th anniversary of the founding of the party, to basically achieve socialist modernisation by 2035, and to build China into a prosperous, strong, democratic, civilised, harmonious and beautiful modern socialist power by the 100th anniversary of the founding of new China, can be further clarified as follows: By the 100th anniversary of the founding of the party, remarkable results are to be achieved through various institutions becoming more mature and more defined; by 2035, various institutions are to be more complete, and the national system of governance and governability will be basically modernised; by the 100th anniversary of the founding of new China, the modernisation of the national system of governance and governability are to be fully accomplished, such that socialism with Chinese characteristics will be more consolidated and its superiority fully demonstrated. The overall requirements and objectives put forward by the plenary session provided the general direction, blueprint and manner of total compliance for upholding socialism with Chinese characteristics in the new era and promoting the modernisation of the national governance system and governability.

The plenary session then also clearly advanced the 13 main tasks pertaining to upholding and perfecting socialism with Chinese characteristics, promoting the modernisation of the national system of governance and governability, and clarified the fundamental points which the various institutions must perfect, uphold, consolidate, and develop, whilst also making arrangements for this work. The plenary session defined the institutions which play the fundamental structural role of "Four Beams and Eight Pillars" within socialism with Chinese characteristics as the fundamental institutions, the basic institutions and the major institutions.

The fundamental institutions refer to those institutions that reflect the essential content and fundamental characteristics of socialism with Chinese characteristics and embody the prescriptions of socialism with Chinese characteristics. These constitute the fundamental basis of statehood and examples of these include the system of party leadership, the institution of the NPC, the fundamental system of Marxism's guiding position in the field of ideology, the absolute leadership of the party over the PLA, and so on.

The basic institutions refer to those that embody the nature of Chinese socialism, frame the basic form of the country, and regulate China's political and economic relations. They include those pertaining to multi-party cooperation and political consultation under the leadership of the CPC, regional ethnic autonomy and grassroots mass autonomy, the basic socialist economic system, and so on.

The major institutions refer to the main institutions of all aspects of national governance derived from the fundamental institutions and the basic institutions, such as the main economic, political, cultural and social institutions, as well as those pertaining to eco-civilisation, military and diplomatic affairs and other fields. This definition furnished by the plenary session constitutes an important institutional arrangement for all aspects of party and state undertakings, and marks the greater systematic, holistic and standardised nature of China's national system and national system of governance. This step also constitutes the clear requirement to strengthen the party's leadership in upholding and perfecting socialism with Chinese characteristics and promoting the modernisation of the national system of governance and governability.

The plenary session emphasised that the construction of the national system and the national system of governance must be carried out under the unified leadership of the CPC Central Committee, and advanced in a united manner with scientific planning, careful organisation, and integrating local and distant concerns to ensure that the objectives set by the plenary session would be fully implemented. The plenary session called on party committees, all levels of government and leading cadres at all levels to take the lead in maintaining institutional authority and serving as a model to lead by example in institutional implementation. The plenary session also proposed clear requirements for strengthening research into institutional theory, publicity and education, improving the ability of cadres in the new era to govern, and the promotion of the comprehensive deepening of reform.

In short, the Fourth Plenary Session of the 19th CPC Central Committee constituted a major groundbreaking and landmark meeting, which will be recorded in the annals of history in connection with the new development of Marxist state doctrine.

(Originally published in the *People's Daily* on 22 November 2019)

CHAPTER FOUR

THE PATH AND ACHIEVEMENTS OF THE FORMATION OF SOCIALISM WITH CHINESE CHARACTERISTICS AND THE NATIONAL SYSTEM OF GOVERNANCE

Marxism tells us that, after seizing power, the proletariat cannot simply use ready-made state apparatus to achieve its own ends, but rather must establish its own political institutions to replace the state apparatus of the ruling class. Socialism with Chinese characteristics and the national system of governance constitute a brand-new state system and national system of governance established by the party after it united and led the people of China to overthrow the reactionary rule of imperialism, feudalism and bureaucratic capitalism. This system, which makes creative use of Marxist state doctrine, profoundly summarises both positive and negative political experiences in China and overseas, and ensures the ownership of the people for China's vast population and was established in the midst of the constant exploration of practice, reform and innovation. It constitutes a great innovation in the history of human institutions and civilisation.

The formation and development of socialism with Chinese characteristics and the national system of governance is based on the valuable experience of the CPC in ruling in the base areas during the period in which it led the New Democratic Revolution and has taken place during the three major historical stages of new China over the past 70 years.

One historical issue facing China in modern times has pertained to the kind of national system which should be established. After the Opium War, countless people with lofty ideals made unremitting efforts to seek a way to change China's prospects and destiny, conducted repeated exploration, and tried a variety of institutional models, but all ended in failure.

Since its establishment, the CPC has devoted itself to the establishment of a new state and society characterised by the ownership of the people, and not only advocated for a future state system, but also led the people to strive for it for more than 20 years, thereby accumulating valuable experience in local governance. Comrade Mao Zedong expounded the institution of the People's Representative Conference at the Second Plenary Session of the seventh CPC Central Committee, pointing out that the parliamentary system of bourgeois republics is not suited to the Chinese situation. Subsequently, in an article entitled *On the People's Democratic Dictatorship*, he clearly stated that: "To sum up our experience, it is concentrated on the people's democratic dictatorship led by the working class (through the CPC) and based on the alliance of workers and peasants." This enabled full theoretical preparations to be made for the construction and development of the new Chinese national system.

In September 1949, the *Common Programme of the Chinese People's Political Consultative Conference* adopted by the First Plenary Session of the CPPCC, established the People's Democratic Dictatorship as the form of government for new China, the institution of the NPC as the political system of new China, the system of multi-party cooperation and political consultation under the leadership of the CPC, and the system of regional ethnic autonomy in a unified multi-ethnic China. These plans executed at the highest level and in comprehensive fashion, lay the foundation of the national system of new China.

In September 1954, the first session of the First National People's Congress was held, marking the formal establishment of the institution of the NPC as the fundamental political system of new China, and subsequently the CPPCC continued to play an important role in the political and social life of the country. The first constitution of new China adopted at this meeting made more comprehensive provisions on the national nature of the people's democratic dictatorship, the fundamental political system of the institution of the NPC, and on the basic political system of the country, such as the systems of multi-party cooperation and political consultation under the leadership of the CPC and the system of regional ethnic autonomy.

In 1956, with the basic completion of the socialist transformation of the private ownership of means of production stipulated by the party's general line in the period of transition, China established basic socialist institutions and successfully achieved the greatest and most profound social transformation in the history of the nation. After that, the party made important progress in exploring a path of development suited to China's national conditions, as well as in institutional construction and construction of the legal system. At one point it also took a wrong turn.

In the following 29 years, the national system established by the people led by the party and the economic foundation which was generally suited to China's actual situation and to the China of that time, despite still being in the immature and imperfect start-up phase, remarkably pioneered the establishment of a new national system characterised by the ownership of the people.

The Third Plenary Session of the 11th CPC Central Committee opened up a new historical period of reform and opening up, as well as a new historical journey of self-improvement and development of socialism with Chinese characteristics. Since then, over the past 40 years, the party has led the people to actively promote the reform of the system of party leadership and economic, political, cultural, social, eco-civilisation-related and military institutions and so on, and constantly improved and developed socialism with Chinese characteristics. In this way, the vitality and efficiency of the national system of governance have been continuously enhanced.

The first goal of the reforms was to improve and perfect the leadership system of the party and the state. At the beginning of the reform and opening up, the local revolutionary committees at all levels established during the Cultural Revolution were abolished and local people's governments at all levels were restored. On the basis of summing up the lessons of the Cultural Revolution, the Fifth Plenary Session of the 11th CPC Central Committee adopted *Some Guidelines on Political Life within the Party* and decided to restore the Secretariat of the Central Committee in order to strengthen and improve the party's collective leadership and democratic centralism. The Constitution enacted in 1982 determined to resume the establishment of the roles of chairman and vice-chairman of the state council and gave the state council the power to make administrative regulations. The state established the central military commission, changed the unified political and social system of the people's communes, and restored the establishment of municipal political organs. The party constitution adopted by the 12th CPC National Congress stipulates that the Party Central Committee shall have only a general secretary and no longer a chairman or vice-chairman. These important measures and regulations are of great significance to the improvement and perfection of the party and state leadership system.

The second goal was to improve and perfect China's fundamental political institutions. In 1982, in accordance with the Constitution, China established standing committees at local people's congresses at or above the county level, giving people's congresses, and their standing committees, in provinces, autonomous regions, and municipalities directly under the Central Government, the power to formulate and promulgate local laws and regulations, as well as implementing changes in the process of electing candidates to the NPC at all levels from a system of single-candidate elections to competitive elections, thereby extending the scope of the direct election of candidates to the county level. The 14th CPC National Congress advanced the strengthening of the NPC's functions and its standing committee in legislation and supervision. The 17th CPC National Congress advanced the gradual implementation of the election of a number of representatives to the NPC in urban and rural areas proportionate to population size. These changes all contributed to the better functioning of the NPC at all levels.

The third goal was to improve and perfect China's basic political institutions. After reform and opening up, the CPC Central Committee further clarified the nature, tasks, themes and functions of the CPPCC and established the system of multi-party cooperation and political consultation under the leadership of the CPC as a basic political system in China. It also provided a new summary of the nature of the democratic parties, clarified the relationship between the ruling party and the participating political parties, and clarified the political norms that multi-party cooperation and political consultation must uphold. The system of grassroots mass autonomy originated from the residents' committees established in China's cities after the founding of new China. In 1982, urban residents' committees and rural villagers' committees were together written into the Constitution. In 1989 and 1998, the *Organic Law of Urban Residents' Committees* and the *Organic Law of Villagers' Committees* were passed in succession. For the first time, the 14th CPC National Congress defined the form of grassroots democracy as the rural villagers' committees, urban residents' committees and enterprise workers' congress, and after that gradually formed a system of grassroots mass autonomy, mainly characterised by these three types of bodies. The system of regional ethnic autonomy, innovatively established by the CPC as a basic political system around the time of the founding of new China, has been continuously enriched and developed in the process of reform and opening up.

The fourth goal was to improve and perfect the basic socialist economic system. The *Decision of the CPC Central Committee on Economic Restructuring* made by the Third Plenary Session of the 12th CPC Central Committee, advanced for the first time the new assertion that the socialist economy is: "a planned commodity economy based on public ownership". The 14th CPC National Congress clearly stated that "the goal of China's economic restructuring is to establish a socialist market economy" and laid a solid institutional foundation for the establishment of the basic socialist economic system. The 15th CPC National Congress proposed for the first time that: "The common development of a multi-ownership economy mainly characterised by public ownership is a basic economic system in the primary stage of socialism in China." This marked the establishment of China's basic socialist economic system.

The fifth goal was to improve and perfect the socialist system of laws with Chinese characteristics. As early as the beginning of the period of reform and opening up, the CPC began to plan and make arrangements to build a legal system with the Constitution as its core. After China in 1982 formulated its first Constitution since the beginning of the period of reform and opening up, it amended the Constitution in 1988, 1993, 1999 and 2004 to incorporate the great achievements and experiences of success created by the people led by the party in the period of reform and opening up. The 15th CPC National Congress identified the rule of law as the basic strategy for governing the country and put forward the goal of forming a socialist legal system with Chinese characteristics by

2010. Under the strong leadership of the CPC Central Committee, this goal has been achieved on schedule.

In the *Decision of the CPC Central Committee on Comprehensively Deepening Reform* adopted by the Third Plenary Session of the 18th CPC Central Committee, the CPC Central Committee, with Comrade Xi Jinping as its core, clearly stated that the overall goal of comprehensively deepening reform is to improve and develop socialism with Chinese characteristics and promote the modernisation of the national system of governance and governability, while also upholding the integration of problem-oriented and goal-oriented approaches in the practice of the comprehensive deepening of reform carried out thenceforth. The *Decision* also actively promoted the construction of party and state institutions and the modernisation of the national system of governance, achieving historic accomplishments. These historic achievements are outlined below.

The *Decision* clearly advanced and promoted the enhancement of the "Four Consciousnesses" the entrenchment of the "Four Matters of Confidence", and the achievement of the "Two Safeguards" throughout the whole party, and consciously maintained a high degree of unity in the party Central Committee with Comrade Xi Jinping as the core in ideology, in politics and in action. The CPC Central Committee set up a number of decision-making and coordinating bodies to improve the system of leadership with regards to major works. The *Decision* improved the system for reporting to the CPC Central Committee. Since 2015, the Secretariat of the Central Committee and the Central Commission for Discipline Inspection, the Party Group of the Standing Committee of the NPC, the Party Group of the State Council, the Party Group of the CPPCC, the Party Group of the Supreme People's Court and the Party Group of the Supreme People's Procuratorate have reported to the Standing Committee of the Politburo of the CPC Central Committee on an annual basis. After the 19th CPC National Congress, party and state institutions were reformed and decisive steps were taken in constructing and perfecting the system of party leadership, the system of governance, the armed forces and the group work system.

The CPC Central Committee advanced and implemented the general requirements for the construction of the party and the party's organisational line in the new era and established and improved the institutional mechanisms for the overall promotion of all aspects of the party's construction, with the political construction of the party as the key priority. The party has improved the system of responsibility for the full and strict control of the party, intensified the party's political discipline and rules, and driven the whole party to resolutely fight against all problems that affect the advancement and weaken the purity of the party. The motions *Some Guidelines on Political Life Within the Party Under the New Situation* and *Some Regulations on the Supervision of the CPC Adopted by the Sixth Plenary Session of the 18th CPC Central Committee*, have promoted a marked improvement in the political ecology within the party. This has led to the establishing of the National Supervisory Commission, improvements in the system of party and state supervision and the strengthening of the restraint and supervision of the exercise of power. The party unswervingly advances the anti-corruption drive and strives to build institutional mechanisms that deter, disenable, and discourage corruption.

UPHOLDING AND IMPROVING THE SOCIALIST LEGAL SYSTEM WITH CHINESE CHARACTERISTICS

The *Decision of the CPC Central Committee on a Few Major Issues Regarding Comprehensive Promotion of the Rule of Law* adopted by the Fourth Plenary Session of the 18th CPC Central

Committee made comprehensive arrangements to build a socialist country ruled by law in the new era, and the construction of the rule of law, in particular reforms of the judicial system, was carried out with unprecedented intensity. After the 19th CPC National Congress, the Law on Supervision, and the Law on National Medals and Honorary Titles was enacted, and legislation was expedited in key areas such as national security, the environment, and society and the welfare of the people, and the socialist legal system with Chinese characteristics was continuously improved.

UPHOLDING AND IMPROVING THE SYSTEM
OF THE OWNERSHIP OF THE PEOPLE

Since the 18th CPC National Congress, the CPC Central Committee has executed designs at the highest level and in comprehensive fashion for upholding and improving the institution of the People's Congress, clearly advanced the leading role to be played by the People's Congress and its Standing Committee in legislative work, set up special social construction committees at all levels of the NPC, and optimised the composition of the Standing Committee of the NPC and the special committees.

Consultative democracy constitutes a distinctive political form and unique strength of China's socialist democratic politics. The CPC Central Committee successively issued and implemented a series of supporting documents, such as *Opinions on Strengthening the Construction of Socialist Consultative Democracy*, leading this form of democracy to be widely used in China's political and social life, effectively guaranteeing the orderly political participation of the people and promoting the scientificisation and democratisation of decision-making.

Since the 18th CPC National Congress, historic progress has also been made in upholding and improving the economic, cultural, and social institutions, as well as those related to eco-civilisation, the military and foreign affairs.

Throughout the whole historical process of socialism from its birth to the present, seizing national power in China, an economically and culturally backward power in East Asia, establishing a socialist system, and then building a modern socialist power, constitutes a brand-new topic in the history of the development of Marxism. How to govern China, a developing socialist country with a long and profound history, extremely large territory and population, a highly complex ethnic structure and an increasingly large-scale economy, constitutes an extremely difficult task for which there are no readily available models from which to learn about the past practice of socialism elsewhere in the world. The CPC has faced up to difficulties, upheld the integration of the basic principles of Marxism with China's concrete reality, and, after arduous exploration, made historic achievements in the construction of the national system in the past 70 years of new China. The Fourth Plenary Session of the 19th CPC Central Committee comprehensively resolved and summarised a full set of institutions for socialism with Chinese characteristics and the national system of governance, mainly encompassing the following aspects.

1. Upholding the centralised and unified leadership of the party and resolutely safeguarding the authority of the CPC Central Committee so that the party will be in the

overall central position to coordinate all parties, and implementing a system of party leadership characterised by scientific, democratic and law-based governance.

2. A system of people's ownership with the institution of the People's Congress as the fundamental political institution, mainly characterised by the basic institutions of the system of multi-party cooperation and political consultation under the leadership of the CPC, the system of regional ethnic autonomy, and the system of grassroots mass autonomy.

3. Unswervingly following the path of the socialist rule of law with Chinese characteristics, a system comprised of a body of legal regulations, and institutions for enforcing, monitoring and guaranteeing the rule of law.

4. Upholding the system of governance in which all administrative organs serve and are accountable and subject to the supervision of the people, which innovates administrative methods, improves administrative efficiency, satisfies the people, has clear responsibilities and conducts administration in accordance with the law.

5. A basic socialist economic system mainly characterised by common economic development featuring multiple types of ownership with public ownership as the main type, and the coexistence of various distribution modes with distribution according to work as the main feature, and a socialist market economy.

6. Upholding the guiding position of Marxism in the field of ideology, persisting in serving the people and socialism, adhering to the important slogan of "let a

hundred flowers bloom; let a hundred schools of thought contend", persisting with creative transformation and innovative development, to stimulate advanced socialist cultural institutions which represent the creative vitality of China's national culture.

7. Persisting in the education of young children, the provision of teachers, ensuring work is remunerated, invalids are treated, the elderly are cared for, people have a place to live, and the weak are supported through integrated urban and rural institutions and systems for protecting people's livelihoods with the goal of meeting people's growing needs for a better life.

8. Leadership of party committees, government responsibility, democratic consultation, social coordination, public participation, protection of the rule of law, scientific and technological support, which together constitute a system for social governance which is co-built and co-governed.

9. Promoting the harmonious coexistence of man and nature, upholding a system of eco-civilisation promoted through joint efforts which upholds environmental protection, efficient use of resources, ecological protection and restoration, and the implementation of the responsibility towards environmental protection.

10. The supreme leadership and command of the PLA belong to the party's Central Committee, and the Central Military Commission implement the chairman responsibility system to ensure a system of the absolute leadership of the party over the PLA with

regards to the nature, purpose and essence of the PLA.

11. Governing the Hong Kong SAR and the Macao SAR in strict accordance with the Constitution and the Basic Law, to maintain the long-term prosperity and stability of Hong Kong and Macao, and to firmly promote "One Country, Two Systems" for the peaceful reunification of the motherland, including Taiwan.

12. Integrated planning for the overall situation within China and overseas, by upholding to an independent and peaceful foreign policy, unswervingly safeguarding national sovereignty, security and developmental interests, unswervingly safeguarding world peace, promoting common development, and advancing diplomatic institutional mechanisms for working to build a community with a "shared future for mankind" .

13. An authoritative and efficient party and state supervisory system with unified party leadership and comprehensive coverage, having as its aim the restraint and supervision of the exercise of power and the achievement of self-purification, self-improvement, self-innovation and self-development.

The national system and the national system of governance constitute the fundamental guarantee for the prosperity of the party and the national cause. In the 70 years since the founding of new China, the CPC has led the Chinese people to write new chapters in the unique Chinese story of socialist revolution and construction, of the new period of reform and opening up, of the historic changes that have taken place since the 18th CPC National Congress, of bringing about the miracles of rapid economic development and long-term social stability, and of the great leap from standing up and getting rich to becoming strong.

Practice has proven that socialism with Chinese characteristics and the national system of governance constitute institutions and a system of governance guided by Marxism, planted in Chinese soil, possessing deep Chinese cultural roots and profoundly experiencing the support of the Chinese people. They also constitute institutions and a system of governance possessing strong vitality and great strength, and which can continuously promote the progress and development of a great power with a population of nearly 1.4 billion people, and ensure that the Chinese nation, with more than 5,000 years of civilisation, achieves the goal of the "Two Centenaries" and thus achieves the great rejuvenation of the Chinese nation.

(Originally published in the *People's Daily* on 2 December 2019)

CHAPTER FIVE

UPHOLDING AND REFINING THE
FUNDAMENTAL INSTITUTIONS OF SOCIALISM
WITH CHINESE CHARACTERISTICS

The fundamental institutions of socialism with Chinese characteristics, together with the basic institutions and the major institutions of socialism with Chinese characteristics, constitute a major political concept that is clearly defined by the Fourth Plenary Session of the 19th CPC Central Committee.

But what exactly are the fundamental institutions of socialism with Chinese characteristics? They are the institutions that embody the intrinsic features of socialism with Chinese characteristics and China's national character, and fundamentally guarantee the direction of, and play a decisive role in, socialism with Chinese characteristics. In order to study and implement the spirit of the Fourth Plenary Session of the 19th CPC Central Committee and uphold and improve the fundamental institutions of socialism with Chinese characteristics, it is necessary to uphold and improve the following institutions and systems.

UPHOLDING AND IMPROVING THE FUNDAMENTAL SYSTEM OF THE LEADERSHIP OF THE PARTY

The leadership of the CPC is the most essential feature, and also the greatest strength of, socialism with Chinese characteristics. Within China's contemporary system of national governance, the CPC constitutes the highest force of political leadership, and the system of party leadership is the "key link" of all party and national institutions, is in the position of overall leadership and command, and constitutes China's most important and most fundamental institution. Without the leadership of the CPC, how could new China have been established, the basic socialist system have been instituted, socialism with Chinese characteristics have been founded, and the set of institutions comprising socialism with Chinese characteristics and the national system of governance have been established, improved and developed?

Upholding and strengthening the overall leadership of the party is closely related to the future and destiny of the party and of China, and errors in this regard tend to be disastrous and subversive. Since the 18th CPC National Congress, the CPC Central Committee, with Comrade Xi Jinping as its core, has comprehensively strengthened and improved the leadership of the party, continuously made robust and perfected the institutional mechanism of the party's leadership, formed a set of institutional norms and working mechanisms which uphold and perfect the party's leadership, and transformed it into an institutional strength for the purposes of national governance, so that socialism with Chinese characteristics will exhibit greater vitality.

The Fourth Plenary Session of the 19th CPC Central Committee systematically summarised the developmental achievements of China's national system and the national system of governance, placed the significant strengths of upholding the leadership of the party at the top of the 13 aspects of China's national system and the national system of governance, and clearly emphasised that: "Regarding the party, politics and the army, the people and education - the party leads everything, and in every corner of the land – north, south, east and west; in order to resolutely safeguard the authority of the party Central Committee, it is necessary to improve the overall national situation and coordinate the system of party leadership, and implement the leadership of the party in all aspects of national governance." The core principle that runs through this is that the system of party leadership constitutes the fundamental institution of socialism with Chinese characteristics. The plenary session gave the highest priority to upholding and improving the system of party leadership, improving the party's scientific and democratic governance, and skill in governance according to law within the context of upholding and improving socialism with Chinese characteristics, and promoting the modernisation of the national system of governance and governability. It thereby underscored the position of the system of party leadership as the fundamental institution within the national system and the national system of governance, and grasped the key to, and fundamental aspects of, the construction of the national system and national governance, ensuring that upholding and strengthening the leadership of the party are more institutionally binding.

Socialism with Chinese characteristics has entered a new era, and socialism with Chinese characteristics and the national system of governance first and foremost need to be continually perfected and developed in keeping with the times in a progressive manner by the system of party leadership. The Fourth Plenary Session of the 19th CPC Central Committee clearly put forward six main tasks based on the system of party leadership with a sound general overview and the coordination of all parties, namely, establishing a system that does not forget the original aspirations and keeps its mission in mind, improving the various institutions for firmly safeguarding the authority of the CPC Central Committee and centralising and unifying leadership, improving the system of comprehensive party leadership, improving various institutions to govern for the people and be governed by the people, improving the party's governing capacity and skill in leadership, and improving the system of party governance in an all-round way.

In order to implement the spirit of the Fourth Plenary Session, it is necessary to give prominence to the implementation of the above six tasks, make greater efforts to uphold and improve the system of party leadership, and stimulate party organisations at all levels and all party and state institutions to embody the leadership of the party in all aspects of national governance, in order to effectively transform the system of party leadership into a strength for the national system and effective national governance.

As the state system and fundamental national system of the People's Republic of China, the people's democratic dictatorship is the product of the creative application and development of the Marxist-Leninist doctrine of the state in China. The "Paris Commune", established in March 1871 in the midst of the stormy proletarian revolution in Paris, constituted the first attempt by the proletariat in France to seize power. Marx and Engels summed up the valuable experience of the Paris Commune and clearly stated that: "After the proletariat seized power, it could not simply use the existing state apparatus to achieve its own aims; it had to establish a state apparatus of the dictatorship of the proletariat to replace the state apparatus of the ruling class." Marx and Engels believed that one of the main reasons for the failure of the Paris Commune was the lack of leadership of the proletarian party, and therefore they specifically proposed that: "In order to unite the working class in the revolutionary struggle, it is necessary to form an independent revolutionary party of the proletariat composed of the advanced elements of the working class and to give full play to the leading role of this party in the revolutionary struggle". Lenin inherited and developed the theory of the dictatorship of the proletariat of Marx and Engels, led the Russian October Revolution to success, and established the first socialist state under the dictatorship of the proletariat in the world, thereby providing an example for other countries to carry out revolution and establish a dictatorship of the proletariat.

The CPC and the Chinese Revolution were established and developed under the guidance of Marxism-Leninism and under the influence of the October Revolution in Russia. The people's democratic dictatorship constitutes a brand-new national system established by the party unifying and leading the Chinese people, after overthrowing the reactionary rule of imperialism, feudalism and bureaucratic capitalism, by creatively applying the Marxist-Leninist theory of the dictatorship of the proletariat in accordance with the historical conditions and specific circumstances of China.

The theoretical proposition of the people's democratic dictatorship was clearly advanced in many official CPC documents and in Mao Zedong's works such as *On New Democracy*, *On United Government*, and *On the People's Democratic Dictatorship*. The practical exploration of the people's democratic dictatorship had already been carried out in the construction of the revolutionary bases before the founding of new China. Mao Zedong emphasised: "To sum up our experience, we have concentrated on the dictatorship of people's democracy led by the working class (through the CPC) on the basis of the alliance of workers and peasants. This dictatorship must be united with the international revolutionary forces. This is our formula, this is our main experience, and this is our main agenda." He also clearly expounded the scientific connotation of the people's democratic dictatorship, stating that: "It is the integration of the democratic aspect of the people and the dictatorship of the reactionary faction which constitutes the people's democratic dictatorship." Practice during the 70 years of new China has proven that the people's democratic dictatorship is a fundamental institution that is in line with China's national conditions, is deeply rooted in the people, and has great vitality and strengths.

The Fourth Plenary Session of the 19th CPC Central Committee emphasised that: "China is a socialist country led by the working class and under the people's democratic dictatorship based on the alliance of workers and peasants", and clearly expressed its firm intention to uphold the people's democratic dictatorship as the country's fundamental institution. The plenary session stressed the prime position of the people, and the necessity of unswervingly following the path of socialist political development with Chinese characteristics, making all institutions and national governance better reflect the will of the people, safeguarding the rights and interests of the people, stimulating innovation by the people, and ensuring that the people manage state affairs through various channels and forms in accordance with the law, and manage economic and cultural undertakings and social affairs. It also clearly advanced the important task of upholding and perfecting the fundamental institution of the people's democratic dictatorship. In a sense, all the institutional arrangements and deployments made by the plenary session to uphold and improve socialism with Chinese characteristics and to promote the modernisation of the national system of governance and governability all constitute the upholding and improvement of the fundamental institution of the people's democratic dictatorship.

UPHOLDING AND IMPROVING THE FUNDAMENTAL INSTITUTION OF THE PEOPLE'S CONGRESS

The institution of the People's Congress is a fundamental institution that conforms to China's national conditions, embodies the essence of a socialist country and ensures the ownership of the people, and is the fundamental institution that supports the national system of governance and governability. As the foundation of the national political system and the organisational framework of state power, the institution of the People's Congress has achieved the organic unity of the state and the government, democracy and efficiency, and constitutes the fundamental institutional arrangement for upholding the organic unity of the leadership of the party, the ownership of the people and the rule of law and embodies the characteristics and strengths of China's socialist democratic politics. The Fourth Plenary Session of the 19th CPC Central Committee fully expounded the status, characteristics and strengths of the fundamental institution of the People's Congress, and clearly advanced the key directions, main tasks, work requirements and important measures for upholding and improving the fundamental institutions of the People's Congress in the coming period.

Firstly, it is vital to support and ensure that the people exercise state power through the People's Congress, ensure that the people at all levels are democratically elected and accountable to and supervised by the people, and ensure that state organs at all levels are elected by, and accountable and subject to supervision by the NPC. This constitutes a requirement for the NPC and its Standing Committees at all levels, as well as for state organs and their staff at all levels. In other words, it is necessary to expand the orderly political participation of citizens from all levels and fields through the People's Congress, to guarantee citizens' right to information, to participate, to expression and to supervise in accordance with the law, and to guarantee the right of all members of society to participate and develop on an equal footing in accordance with the law. At the same time, it is necessary to open channels of reflection and expression of public opinion, actively respond to social concerns, take into account different interests, maximise the mobilisation of positive factors, and resolve negative factors.

Secondly, it is vital to support and ensure that the NPC and its Standing Committee exercise their legislative power in accordance with the law, improve the socialist legal system with Chinese characteristics with the Constitution as its core, strengthen legislation in important areas, uphold scientific, democratic and legal legislation, and continuously improve the quality and efficiency of legislation, as well as exercise the power of supervision in accordance with the law, perfect the supervision system of the NPC over the system of "One Government, One Committee, Two Chambers", strengthening supervision over the implementation of the law, ensuring that administrative, supervisory, judicial and procuratorial power are properly exercised in accordance with the law, ensuring that the legitimate rights and interests of citizens, legal persons and other organisations are effectively protected, and resolutely eliminating interference in law enforcement and judicial activities. Additionally, it is vital to ensure that the NPC and its Standing Committee exercise the right to make decisions in accordance with the law, and discuss and make decisions regarding major matters nationally and in administrative regions in accordance with the Constitution and the relevant organic law, as well as exercise the right of appointment and dismissal in accordance with the law and elect and dismiss the leaders, members and staff of state organs in strict accordance with statutory powers and procedures.

Thirdly, it is vital to foster close contact between NPC delegates and the people, improve the mechanism for liaising between delegates, and better demonstrate the role of NPC delegates. On the one hand, NPC deputies at all levels should, through research, inspections, visits, delegate liaison points, delegate meeting rooms, and delegates welcome days, network platforms and other methods and channels, understand public sentiment, reflect the demands of the masses, and promote national laws, regulations and policies. On the other hand, the Standing Committee of the NPC at all levels should also improve the system of contact between delegates, provide support and ensure that delegates perform their duties in accordance with the law, and make full use of the role of delegates.

Fourthly, it is vital to improve the organisational system, electoral system and the rules of procedure of the NPC, and improve the system of argumentation, assessment, evaluation and hearings. According to the requirements of the party Central Committee, it is necessary to summarise experience from practice, adapt to the new situation and new requirements, improve the legal system regarding the NPC organisational system, working mechanism, and rules of procedure, and improve the NPC organisational system and operational mechanism, so that the NPC and its Standing Committee at all levels become working organs which are fully responsible for the duties entrusted to constitutional law and representative organs which maintain close contact with the people.

UPHOLDING AND IMPROVING FUNDAMENTAL INSTITUTIONS PERTAINING TO THE GUIDING POSITION OF MARXISM IN THE FIELD OF IDEOLOGY

Marxism, with its scientific world outlook and methodology, reveals the law of development of human society, and is the fundamental guiding ideology for the establishment of the party and the state. The CPC grew and developed under the guidance of Marxism and armed forces, the party's advanced nature and purity were formed and enriched under the advanced and scientific nourishment of Marxist ideological theory, and the unity and powerful combat force of the party were assembled and strengthened on the basis of Marxism which constitutes the common ideology of the whole party. In the final analysis, all the achievements from the party-led Chinese revolution, construction, and reform were all accomplished under the guidance of Marxism and the Sinicisation of Marxism in China. Significantly, the Fourth Plenary Session of the 19th CPC Central Committee elevated the guiding position of Marxism to the position of a fundamental system in the field of ideology, objectively exhibiting the great historical role played by Marxism after its introduction into China and establishing by institutional form the fundamental institutional position of Marxist guiding ideology within socialism with Chinese characteristics.

In order to uphold and improve the fundamental system of the guiding position of Marxism in the field of ideology, the most important thing is to uphold and consolidate the national and party guiding ideology of Xi Jinping Thought on Socialism with Chinese Characteristics for a New Era. Xi Jinping Thought on Socialism with Chinese Characteristics for a New Era is the latest achievement in the Sinicisation of Marxism and constitutes contemporary Chinese Marxism and 21st century Marxism. It has furnished guidelines for scientific action for the establishment of a strong party and nation and national rejuvenation and has provided a powerful ideological weapon for the party and the people.

In accordance with the requirements of learning, gaining a firm grasp of matters, and being realistic, it is vital to further promote the study of Xi Jinping Thought on Socialism with

Chinese Characteristics for a New Era, guide party members and cadres to deeply understand the historical status and significance of this ideology, deeply comprehend the spiritual essence, rich content, core meaning and practical requirements of this ideology, deeply understand the Marxist position, viewpoint and methodology which permeate it, and truly translate the harvest of learning this ideology into concrete action to enhance the "Four Consciousnesses", stabilise the "Four Matters of Confidence" and accomplish the "Two Safeguards", and to translate it into ideas, initiatives and scientific methods in order to work well.

Upholding and perfecting the fundamental system of the guiding position of Marxism in the field of ideology requires the party to firmly grasp the direction of advanced socialist culture and strengthen the overall leadership of the party in ideological work. Now, China's cultural field is undergoing extensive and profound changes, the socio-cultural ecology is more complex, and so the importance of upholding Marxism to lead the development of diversified culture is increasingly evident. To this end it is vital to uphold the unswerving management by the party of propaganda, ideology and the media, place leadership in ideological work firmly in the hands of those loyal to the party and to Marxism, and constantly enhance the dominant power and voice of the field of ideology.

The Fourth Plenary Session of the 19th CPC Central Committee clearly proposed upholding the guiding position of Marxism in the field of ideology, and that it is crucial to pay attention to distinguishing between issues of political principle, of ideological understanding and of academic perspectives, and clearly oppose and resist all kinds of wrong ideas. This requirement is very important but also very relevant to reality.

On this important issue, we must persist in seeking truth from facts, objectivity and impartiality, persevere with concrete analysis of specific problems, and identify problems for what they really are. Then we must solve problems of a particular nature in the appropriate way, and not only prevent academic perspectives, and in particular issues of ideological under-standing, from being elevated to the level of issues pertaining to political principles, but also prevent issues pertaining to political principles from being diluted down to the level of academic perspectives or ideological understanding.

UPHOLDING AND IMPROVING THE FUNDAMENTAL SYSTEM OF THE ABSOLUTE LEADERSHIP OF THE PARTY OVER THE PLA

The PLA is a strong pillar of socialism with Chinese characteristics. The absolute leadership of the party over the PLA constitutes an essential characteristic of socialism with Chinese characteristics, an important political strength of the party and the state, and the foundation of the PLA and the soul of a strong army. The Fourth Plenary Session of the 19th CPC Central Committee took "adherence to the party's command of the gun" as a significant strength of China's national system and national system of governance and elevated the "absolute leadership of the party over the PLA" to the status of a fundamental system of socialism with Chinese characteristics, making scientific arrangements for this. This is of great and far-reaching significance for the consolidation the party's ruling position, ensuring the ownership of the people, and achieving the long-term stability of the party and the country.

The fundamental system of the absolute leadership of the party over the PLA originated from the party's feat at the Nanchang Uprising of independently leading a new type of people's army, and was founded on the creation of the principle of "party branches organised at the company level" in the Sanwan Reformation. It was established at the Gutian Conference on the principle of building the party with ideology and the PLA with politics and was enriched and developed in the great practice of the party leading the PLA in revolution, construction and reform.

For more than 90 years, the PLA has endured various tests and hundreds of battles, large and small. The reason why it has struggled hard but not collapsed is because it has become more and more resilient after repeated setbacks and has won decisive battles. In all of this the most fundamental aspect has been the strong leadership of the party. Without this absolute leadership of the party over the PLA, there could have been no liberation of the people and no national independence. On 5 March 1949, Mao Zedong said at the Second Plenary Session of the Seventh Central Committee: "The People's Republic is founded on the PLA; Chiang Kai-shek's kingdom fell due to the fall of his army."

In the new era, upholding and perfecting the fundamental system of the absolute leadership of the party over the PLA constitutes an important part of uphold and perfecting socialism with Chinese characteristics, promoting the modernisation of the national system of governance and governability, and also a strong guarantee for realising the Chinese dream and the dream of having a strong military. The world today is undergoing great changes not seen in a hundred years, and China is in a critical period of realising the great rejuvenation of the Chinese nation. Facing the demands of the times for having a powerful state and powerful military, and facing profound changes in the national security environment, it is vital to keep pace with the times to enrich and perfect the fundamental system of the absolute leadership of the party over the PLA. Only in this way will we be able to transform the political and organisational strengths of the party into a winning edge, ensure that the construction and use of military force better meet the risks and challenges ahead, achieve greater compliance with the highest and fundamental interests of serving the great rejuvenation of the Chinese nation, and thereby faithfully fulfil the mission of the new era entrusted by the party and the people.

In order to uphold and perfect the fundamental system of the absolute leadership of the party over the PLA, the most basic thing is that the military must be placed unconditionally under the leadership of the party, always maintain a high degree of consistency with the CPC Central Committee and the Central Military Commission in ideology, politics, and action, resolutely safeguard the authority of the CPC Central Committee and the Central Military Commission, and resolutely obey the command of the CPC Central Committee and the Central Military Commission at all times and in all situations. The most important thing in this regard is to firmly uphold the belonging of the supreme leadership and command of the PLA to the CPC Central Committee and fully and profoundly implement the chairmanship of the Military Commission.

The Fourth Plenary Session of the 19th CPC Central Committee made it clear that the guiding position in national defence and military construction of Xi Jinping's ideology on a strong military must be firmly established, that the national armed forces should be under the unified leadership and command of the chairman of the Military Commission, that the institutional mechanism for implementing the chairmanship of the Military Commission should be improved, and that major measures required by the institutional regulations of the chairmanship of the Military Commission should be strictly implemented. This has a fundamental role to play in ensuring the absolute leadership of the party over the PLA, realising the party's goal of a having a strong military in the new era, and forever maintaining the nature, purpose and character of the PLA.

To sum up, the fundamental institutions of the leadership of the party, the people's democratic dictatorship, the People's Congress, the guiding position of Marxism in the field of ideology, and the absolute leadership of the party over the PLA play the role of the "main beam" and "top pillar" in the fundamental "Four Beams and Eight Pillars" structure of China's national system and the national system of governance, and fundamentally embody the institutional strengths of socialism with Chinese characteristics. In order to learn and implement the spirit of the Fourth Plenary Session of the 19th CPC Central Committee, it is vital to establish an awareness of the fundamental institutions, to only consolidate and never destabilise them, and to only improve and never weaken them.

(Originally published in the *Study Times* on 29 November 2019)

CHAPTER SIX

UPHOLDING AND REFINING THE BASIC INSTITUTIONS OF SOCIALISM WITH CHINESE CHARACTERISTICS

The basic institutions of socialism with Chinese characteristics are those which embody China's socialist nature, stipulate the basic principles of its political and economic life, and have a great impact on the country's economic and social development. In order to implement the spirit of the Fourth Plenary Session of the 19th CPC Central Committee, it is necessary to uphold and improve the following basic systems and institutions of socialism with Chinese characteristics.

The basic political system of multi-party cooperation and political consultation under the leadership of the CPC constitutes the inevitable outcome of the historical, theoretical, and practical logic of the long struggle of the Chinese people in modern times, the distinctive form and unique strength of China's socialist political system, and the great political creation of the CPC, the Chinese people and the democratic parties and non-partisans. This basic political system is able to truly, extensively and continuously represent and realise the fundamental interests of the vast majority of the people and of all ethnic groups across China, and effectively avoid the systemic problems of the old-style political party system on behalf of minorities and minority interest groups. It is also able to closely unite the various political parties and non-partisans in order to strive for common goals and has not only effectively prevented the lack of supervision of one-party rule, but also effectively avoided the systemic shortcomings of internal strife from mutual rejection and vicious competition inevitably resulting from Western multi-party systems. In addition, it is also able to broadly focus on various opinions and suggestions through institutionalised, procedural and standardised arrangements, promote the scientificisation and democratisation of decision-making, and effectively avoid the systemic problems of the old-style political party system which led to the laceration of society by decision-making and governance based on party, class, regional and group interests.

To sum up, this basic political system fully manifests the distinctive features of the leadership of the CPC and multi-party cooperation, the governance of the CPC and multi-party participation in politics and reflects the essence of socialist democracy in the ownership of the people in China. Just as General Secretary Xi Jinping pointed out, the institution of multi-party cooperation and political consultation under the leadership of the CPC as a basic political institution in China, is not only in line with the reality of contemporary China, but also in line with the excellent traditional culture of the Chinese nation, which has always advocated that the world constitutes a commonwealth and advocated for inclusion and integration, and seeking common ground while preserving differences. This system constitutes a great contribution to human political civilisation.

The Constitution of the PRC clearly states that: "The system of multi-party cooperation and political consultation will exist and develop for a long time." The Fourth Plenary Session of the 19th CPC Central Committee made clear the major principles that must be firmly upheld, and made new institutional designs and arrangements for upholding and improving this basic political system. In order to implement the requirements of the plenary session, it is necessary to effectively implement the policy of long-term coexistence, mutual supervision, mutual care and sharing of weal and woe, strengthen the construction of the socialist political party system with Chinese characteristics, give full play to the role of democratic parties and non-partisans in participating in and deliberating on politics and democratic supervision, and improve the mechanisms for mutual supervision. It is also necessary to ensure sound mutual supervision, in particular the CPC's conscious acceptance of supervision and special supervision of the implementation of major decisions and arrangements and improve the system of the central committees of democratic parties making proposals directly to the CPC Central Committee, improve the methods of supporting democratic parties and non-partisans in performing their functions, and display the strengths of China's new political party system.

The CPPCC is an important institution under the leadership of the CPC for multi-party cooperation and political consultation, and an important political and organisational form for the implementation of China's new political party system. The CPPCC at all levels should support all democratic parties and non-partisans to participate in the discussion and consultation of major national policies and guidelines in the CPPCC, make institutional arrangements for the democratic parties to express their views and make proposals at the CPPCC on behalf of their respective parties, and effectively create conditions for the democratic parties to perform their duties. Since the 18th CPC National Congress, the CPPCC at all levels has achieved significant progress and results in improving the consultative and deliberative pattern of the CPPCC, with plenary sessions as the leading feature and thematic standing committee meetings, thematic consultation meetings, and consultative symposiums as the focus. It is vital to build on the momentum and continue to improve and develop. In particular, it is necessary to support the democratic parties and non-partisans in political consultation on national policy and important local initiatives, as well as economic, political, cultural, social, eco-civilisation and other important issues, to engage in full consultation and discussion, express their views, criticism and suggestions. The CPPCC Standing Committee meetings and other methods of discussion and work should also improve the consultation and supervision of the common affairs of all parties participating in the CPPCC and important internal affairs of the CPPCC, in order to make full use of the role of the democratic parties.

UPHOLDING AND IMPROVING THE BASIC POLITICAL
SYSTEM OF REGIONAL ETHNIC AUTONOMY

The basic political system of regional ethnic autonomy is a system for the local implementation of regional autonomy, the establishment of autonomous organs and the exercise of autonomy in places where ethnic minorities live. This basic political system constitutes the creative institutional arrangement of the CPC to solve ethnic issues in China.

China has been a unified multi-ethnic country since ancient times, and all ethnic groups have jointly developed China's vast territory, written China's long history, created China's splendid culture, and nurtured the great national spirit of the Chinese people. The diversity of the Chinese nation and China's multi-ethnic unity are valuable political assets handed down and inherited from the more than 5,000 year history of the development of China's civilisation and constitute a great strength of the development and progress of China. By combining Marxist ethnic theory with the multi-ethnic reality of a unified China, the CPC has creatively explored the correct path for solving China's ethnic issues and developed this unique form of regional ethnic autonomy in places where ethnic minorities live.

China's system of regional ethnic autonomy has always been strongly guaranteed by the Constitution and the law. In 1949, the system of regional ethnic autonomy was established in the *Common Programme of the CPPCC*, which served as an interim constitution. The First National People's Congress held in 1954 enshrined the system of regional ethnic autonomy in the *Constitution of the PRC*. *The Law of the PRC on Regional Ethnic Autonomy*, as amended in 2001, clearly stipulates the system of regional ethnic autonomy as one of China's basic political systems. The 19th CPC National Congress elevated the adherence to and refining of the system of regional ethnic autonomy to the level of a basic strategy for upholding and developing socialism with Chinese characteristics in the new era.

The Fourth Plenary Session of the 19th CPC Central Committee recognised "upholding the equality of all ethnic groups, establishing a strong sense of community for the Chinese nation, and realising the common struggle for unity and common prosperous development" as a significant strength of China's national system and national system of governance, and made arrangements and deployments for upholding and perfecting the system of regional ethnic autonomy in the new era. At present, with five autonomous regions, thirty autonomous prefectures, 120 autonomous counties (banners), and nearly 1,000 ethnic townships in China constituting an important supplementary form of regional ethnic autonomy, China's system of regional ethnic autonomy has been continuously enriched, refined and developed. Practice has fully proven that the system of regional ethnic autonomy is suited to China's national conditions and plays an important role in safeguarding national unity and territorial integrity, strengthening ethnic equality and unity, promoting the development of ethnic regions and enhancing Chinese national cohesiveness. In order to implement the arrangements made by the plenary session, it is necessary to firmly establish institutional confidence, always to firmly take the correct and uniquely Chinese path to resolving ethnic issues, and always to uphold and constantly improve the system of regional ethnic autonomy at all times.

In order to uphold and improve the system of regional ethnic autonomy, it is first of all necessary to uphold the equality of all ethnic groups, uphold the common struggle for the unity of all ethnic groups and common prosperous development, ensure that ethnic autonomous regions exercise their right to self-government in accordance with the law, safeguard the legitimate rights and interests of ethnic minorities, and consolidate and develop socialist ethnic relations characterised by equality, solidarity, mutual assistance and harmony. It is vital always to uphold the overall leadership of the CPC, uphold the integration of unification and autonomy and ethnic and regional factors, uphold the rule of law, and promote harmonious coexistence, striving for the same cause and development of all ethnic groups in order to together achieve the great rejuvenation of the Chinese nation.

Secondly, it is vital to persistently implement publicity and education regarding the Marxist views of the fatherland, nationality, culture and history, and constantly enhance the recognition of the various ethnic groups of the great motherland, the Chinese nation, Chinese culture, the CPC, and socialism with Chinese characteristics in order to strengthen the ideological foundations of the Chinese national community. It is also necessary to profoundly and permanently develop the progressive creation of national unity in order to strengthen the interaction and exchange of ethnic groups.

Thirdly, it is vital to support and assist the accelerated development of ethnic regions, organically integrate policy dynamics and endogenous potential, make full use of the initiative of the central government, developed regions and ethnic regions, implement differentiated regional policies for border areas, poor regions and ecological protection zones, optimise institutional mechanisms for transfer payments and counterpart support, implement plans to promote the development of ethnic regions and less populous ethnic groups, revitalise border areas and enrich the lives of inhabitants, focus on employment and education and on ensuring local resources benefit local areas, on protecting the ecology, on poverty alleviation in poor areas and groups with special difficulties, and on infrastructure and opening up to the outside, and continuously improve the living standards of the people of all ethnic groups.

UPHOLDING AND IMPROVING THE BASIC POLITICAL SYSTEM OF GRASSROOTS MASS AUTONOMY

The basic political system of grassroots mass autonomy is a system in which the masses, under the leadership of the party, exercise democratic management over public affairs and public welfare undertakings, as well as enterprises and institutions at the level of rural villages and urban communities. This system began with the establishment of residents' committees in China's cities after the founding of new China. In 1982, the urban residents' committees and the rural villagers' committees were together written into the Constitution. In 1989 and 1998, the *Organic Law of the Urban Residents' Committees of the PRC* and the *Organic Law of the Villagers' Committees of the PRC* were successively adopted. In 1992, the 14th CPC Party Congress for the first time defined China's grassroots democratic system as being comprised of rural villagers' committees, urban residents' committees and enterprise workers' representative assemblies, and since then a basic political system of grassroots mass autonomy has gradually formed, mainly characterised by villagers' committees, residents' committees and workers' representative assemblies.

Villagers' autonomy is a system in which farmers directly exercise their democratic rights and conduct their own affairs in accordance with the law, and the Constitution stipulates the legal status of villagers' committees as mass organisations for the purposes of rural grassroots autonomy. Urban residents' committees are organisations for the purpose of urban grassroots mass autonomy in China, and also an important mode of achieving direct democracy at the grassroots level in cities.

Under the leadership of the CPC, the autonomous committees of villagers and urban residents achieve democratic elections, democratic decision-making, democratic management and democratic supervision, as well as self-management, self-service, self-education and self-monitoring. They also handle public affairs and public welfare in local residential areas, mediate in civil disputes, assist in maintaining social order, and, through committees established for civil mediation, law and order and public health, convey the opinions, demands and suggestions of the people to the People's Government. The system of workers' representative assemblies is a system to ensure that workers can exercise democratic management in enterprises and institutions, and it is the basic institutional mode for the employees of enterprises and institutions to participate in management, to ensure their right to information, participation, expression and supervision, and safeguard their legitimate rights and interests.

The basic political system of grassroots mass autonomy in China, consisting mainly of the autonomy of villagers and urban residents, and workers' representative assemblies in enterprises and institutions, is organically connected with the basic political systems and institutions of the People's

Congress, multi-party cooperation and political consultation under the leadership of the CPC, and regional ethnic autonomy, which together constitute the system of the ownership of the people. In this way, China's characteristic national system of the ownership of the people is reflected not only at the level of state affairs and economic and cultural undertakings, but also at the level of social affairs; not only at the level of people's representative democracy, but also at the level of direct democracy at the grassroots level. All of this has strongly demonstrated the significant strengths and unique characteristics of China's socialist democracy, and fully demonstrated the breadth and authenticity of China's socialist democracy.

Since the 18th Party Congress, with the rapid development of China's industrialisation and urbanisation, China's urban and rural interests have been profoundly adjusted, and a series of new problems have emerged in urban and rural social management. The Fourth Plenary Session of the 19th CPC Central Committee clearly put forward, with the new reality as the point of departure, new requirements and new tasks to improve the system of grassroots mass autonomy.

The first task is to improve the mechanisms of grassroots mass autonomy led by grassroots party organisations. In this regard, the secretaries of party organisations of urban and rural communities should be appointed as the heads of the village (neighbourhood) committee through statutory procedures, and the two village (neighbourhood) committees should be cross-posted so that CPC members have a controlling proportion among the members of the village (neighbourhood) committee and village (neighbourhood) representatives, in order to embody the leading role of grassroots party organisations in all aspects, areas, and sectors of grassroots mass autonomy.

The second task is to work hard to promote the institution-alisation, standardisation, and programmatisation of direct democracy at the grassroots level. To this end it is necessary to establish robust and appropriate institutions to guarantee the electoral rights of the (neighbourhood) villagers and the implementation of democratic elections, and to ensure elections are open, fair and impartial. Also necessary is the establishment of a robust system and mechanism for consultation and decision-making, in order to guarantee the (neighbourhood) villagers' right to discuss and decide on major village (neighbourhood) affairs.

The third task is to improve the democratic management system of enterprises and institutions with workers' representative assemblies as the basic mode. To this end it is necessary to explore effective ways for enterprise workers to participate in management, to protect the rights of the workforce to information, participation, expression, and supervision, and safeguard the legitimate rights and interests of workers.

UPHOLDING AND IMPROVING THE BASIC SOCIALIST ECONOMIC SYSTEM

The basic socialist economic system mainly includes three basic elements: ownership of the means of production, mode of distribution and mode of resource allocation, which is a long-term and stable part of the economic system and has a decisive impact on the attributes of the economic system and the mode of economic development. After the founding of new China, the situation faced by China is neither the construction of socialism on the basis of highly developed capitalism as envisioned by the founders of Marxism, nor is it exactly the same as other socialist countries. Therefore, it is vital to integrate the basic principles of Marxism with the specific reality of China, pioneer the path of socialism with Chinese characteristics in practice, and establish a robust basic socialist economic system with Chinese characteristics. On this issue, the CPC has made profitable explorations, achieved historic results, and experienced twists and turns.

Since the Third Plenary Session of the 11th CPC Central Committee, the CPC has deeply summarised both positive and negative experiences both within China and overseas, and, starting from the basic national conditions of the primary stage of socialism in China, has emancipated people's minds and sought truth from facts. The CPC has achieved the transformation from a single public economy to the common development of an economy with multiple types of ownership where public ownership predominates, from a single method of distribution to a system with multiple methods of distribution where distribution by labour predominates, and from a highly centralised planned economy to a socialist market economy where the market plays a decisive role in resource allocation and which makes better use of the role of the government. This has greatly liberated and developed social productivity, greatly enhanced social vitality, and created the rarely seen miraculous occurrence of rapid economic development and long-term social stability.

The Fourth Plenary Session of the 19th CPC Central Committee, from the level of the national system and the national system of governance, regarded "upholding the common development of an economy with multiple types of ownership where public ownership predominates and multiple methods of distribution where distribution by labour predominates, organically integrating the socialist system with the market economy, and constantly liberating and developing social productivity" as a significant strength of socialism with Chinese characteristics, whilst also elevating multiple methods of distribution where distribution by labour predominates and the socialist market economy to the status of basic socialist economic system. This constitutes a new overview of the basic socialist economic system and a major expansion and deepening of the implications of the basic socialist economic system, as well as the full affirmation of the great practical achievements and great accomplishments of China's economic system reforms over the past 40 years of reform and opening up using institutional forms and has great theoretical and practical significance.

Socialism with Chinese characteristics has entered a new era, but the basic situation that China is in and will remain in for a long time, namely the primary stage of socialism, remains unchanged, and China's status internationally as the largest developing country in the world is still unchanged. Economic construction is still the centre of all the work of the party and the state and liberating and developing social productivity is still the fundamental task of the party and the state, and concentrating on construction and single-mindedly seeking development is still the first priority of the CPC within the context of governing and rejuvenating China. This requires the CPC to follow the arrangements made by the Fourth Plenary Session of the 19th CPC Central Committee to fully implement basic party theory, line and strategy, always uphold economic construction as the central focus, and, as always, regard development as the first priority, continuing to unswervingly and comprehensively deepen reform.

General Secretary Xi Jinping pointed out that: "The economic base determines the superstructure. The reform of the economy has an important impact, and a conductive effect, on the reform of other areas. The progress of economic reform determines the progress of the reform of many other systems, and slight changes in the economy impact everything else." He also pointed out that: "In the comprehensive deepening of reform, we must uphold economic reform as the principle focal point and strive to make new breakthroughs in important areas and key aspects of reform, so as to propel and drive forward other areas of reform, to make all aspects of reform synergistic and create synergies, rather than being fragmented and scattered efforts."

We should conscientiously implement General Secretary Xi Jinping's demand, and, in the practice of the overall promotion of the 13 tasks of building the national system and the national system of governance, which was put in place at the Fourth Plenary Session of the 19th CPC Central Committee, give full play to the common development of an economy with multiple types of ownership where public ownership predominates and multiple methods of distribution where distribution by labour predominates and the leading role of the basic socialist economic system, such as with regards to the socialist market economy, in overall system reform and institutional construction. Through the reform of the economic system and the construction of economic infrastructure we should drive and support the change and improvement of the superstructure, in order to more fully reflect the superiority and strong vitality of the socialist system.

(Originally published in the *Study Times* on 2 December 2019)

CHAPTER SEVEN

UPHOLDING AND REFINING THE MAJOR INSTITUTIONS OF THE SOCIALIST RULE OF LAW WITH CHINESE CHARACTERISTICS

The major institutions of socialism with Chinese characteristics are the main institutions in various fields of national governance derived from the fundamental institutions of socialism with Chinese characteristics and the basic institutions of socialism with Chinese characteristics, specifically including the main institutions pertaining to the rule of law, administration, cultural construction, livelihood protection, social governance, eco-civilisation, "One Country, Two Systems", diplomatic affairs, and party and state supervision, which are built on the fundamental institutions and the basic institutions. The major institutions of socialism with Chinese characteristics connect to the top level of the national system of governance, namely the fundamental institutions and basic institutions, and extend downward to all aspects of social and productive life, so that the overall requirements and objectives of national governance and a series of policy initiatives are implemented in detail, and the strengths of socialism with Chinese characteristics and the functionality of the national system of governance are brought fully into play.

UPHOLDING AND IMPROVING THE MAJOR
INSTITUTIONS OF THE SOCIALIST SYSTEM OF
GOVERNANCE WITH CHINESE CHARACTERISTICS

Building the system of the socialist rule of law with Chinese characteristics and building a socialist state under the rule of law, is an inherent requirement for upholding and developing socialism with Chinese characteristics. Over the past 40 years of reform and opening up, the CPC has persisted in making the rule of law the basic strategy for the party to lead the people in governing the country and on making governance according to the law the basic way for the party to govern the country, continuously enriching and refining the major institutions of the socialist rule of law with Chinese characteristics and providing a strong guarantee for the development and progress of contemporary China. Practice has proven that reform, development and stability cannot be separated from the role of the rule of law as a powerful escort, that economic and social development depends on the empowerment of the rule of law, and that the security and well-being of the people depends on the guardians of the rule of law.

Law is the most important institutional form and the highest form of institution. In order to uphold and refine the major institutions of the socialist rule of law with Chinese characteristics, it is necessary to comprehensively promote scientific legislation, strict law enforcement, impartial justice, the construction of a system for universal compliance with the law and an intraparty regulatory system.

With regards to legislation, in order to provide the basic foundation for the comprehensive rule of law, it is necessary to continuously improve the quality and efficiency of legislation, and constantly refine laws, administrative regulations, local laws and regulations, as well as support institutional provisions and accelerate the formation of a complete legal system.

With regards to law enforcement, it is necessary to uphold adherence to the law, strict law enforcement, and investigations of violations of the law, strictly regulate fair and civilised law enforcement, standardise discretionary powers for law enforcement, and increase law enforcement efforts in key areas of vital interest to the public.

With regards to the judiciary, it is necessary to deepen comprehensive reforms of the judicial system, refine the trial and prosecutorial systems, fully implement judicial accountability, refine the system of lawyers, strengthen the supervision of judicial activities, accelerate the formation of an efficient system for the implementation of the rule of law and ensure the full and effective implementation of laws and regulations.

In terms of compliance with the law, it is necessary to intensify work to improve legal literacy and enhance the concept of the rule of law amongst the whole population, refine the system of public legal services, and consolidate the mass foundation of the rule of law.

With regards to the intraparty regulatory system, it is necessary to persist in ensuring party rules and regulations are stricter than national laws, focus on the convergence and coordination of party regulations and national laws, accelerate the formation of a sound intraparty regulatory system, and give full play to the leading and guaranteeing role of governing the party in accordance with the rules in the work of national governance by the rule of law.

It is necessary to improve legislation, law enforcement, and constraints in the exercising of judicial power and supervision mechanisms, as well as strengthen the construction of intraparty supervision, supervision of the NPC, and administrative, democratic, judicial, audit and social supervision and public opinion monitoring, in addition to accelerating the formation of a rigorous system for the supervision of the rule of law, and enhancing the synergy and effectiveness of supervision.

UPHOLDING AND IMPROVING THE MAJOR INSTITUTIONS OF THE SOCIALIST SYSTEM OF GOVERNANCE WITH CHINESE CHARACTERISTICS

The system of governance assumes the major responsibilities of promoting economic and social development, managing social affairs and serving the people in accordance with the decisions and arrangements of the party and the state, and constitutes an important part of the national system and the national system of governance.

The Fourth Plenary Session of the 19th CPC Central Committee made "upholding and refining the socialist administrative system with Chinese characteristics and building a system of governance with clear responsibilities and administered in accordance with the law" a major task in the construction of the national system and the national system of governance, reflecting the crucial requirement of promoting the modernisation of the national system of governance and governability.

In the new era, in order to uphold and refine the major institutions of the socialist system of governance with Chinese characteristics, it is first necessary to refine the state administrative system by optimising the systems of administrative decision-making, implementation, organisation and supervision, and improving mechanisms for sound departmental cooperation and coordination, in order to prevent multiple policies and policy effects from offsetting each other, by focusing on promoting the optimisation of the functions of state institutions, synergy and efficiency, and being guided by the modernisation of the national system of governance and governability.

Secondly, it is necessary to optimise the system of government responsibilities, by improving the relevant systems and mechanisms, improving the government's economic regulation, market supervision, social management, public services, ecological and environmental protection and other functions, implementing the government's system for listing rights and responsibilities, clarifying the relationship between the government and the market and the government and society, improving the government's executive powers and credibility, and building a service-oriented government able to satisfy the people.

Thirdly, it is necessary to optimise the government's organisational structure by promoting the legalisation of institutions, functions, powers, procedures, and responsibilities, so that government agencies will be more scientific and more functionally optimised with greater synergy of authority and responsibility, able to effectively perform the administrative functions of the state.

Fourthly, it is necessary to ensure sound institutional mechanisms to give full play to both central and local initiative by rationalising the relationship between central and local powers and responsibilities, strengthening the central management of macro affairs, and maintaining the unity of the national legal system, government decrees, and the market. In this regard, more autonomy should be given locally to support local creative work and, in accordance with the principle of consistent authority and responsibility, vertical and local hierarchical management systems should be standardised. In addition, it is vital to build a work system from the central to the local level with clear structures of authority and responsibility, which runs smoothly, and is dynamic.

UPHOLDING AND REFINING THE MAJOR INSTITUTIONS OF SOCIALIST CULTURE WITH CHINESE CHARACTERISTICS

Socialist culture with Chinese characteristics constitutes profound support for the modernisation of the national system of governance and governability. The excellent Chinese traditional culture nurtured in the development of civilisation for more than 5,000 years and the revolutionary culture and advanced socialist culture nurtured in the great struggle of the CPC and the Chinese people have accumulated the deepest spiritual pursuits of, and represent the unique spiritual identity of, the Chinese nation. In order to promote socialist culture with Chinese characteristics, not only is it necessary to depend on the guidance of education and the nurturing provided by practice, but also the guarantees provided by systems and institutional mechanisms.

In this regard it is necessary to uphold and refine core socialist values to lead the institutions for cultural construction. First of all, it is vital to uphold the common ideals of socialism with Chinese characteristics and vigorously promote the national spirit with patriotism as its core and the zeitgeist with reform and innovation as its core, in order to guide the people to deeply understand the realistic basis and bright prospects for achieving the great rejuvenation of the Chinese nation, and firmly establish the "Four Matters of Confidence".

It is also necessary to uphold the integration of the rule of law and the rule of virtue, refine and promote the legal policy system based on core socialist values, integrate the requirements of the core values into the construction of the rule of law and social governance, advance into the whole process of the creation, production and dissemination of spiritual and cultural products, and enhance people's recognition and practice of core values.

To this end a sound system for the protection of people's cultural rights and interests is essential. On the one hand, it is necessary to uphold a people-centred work orientation, refine the mechanisms for guidance and incentives for the creation, production and dissemination of cultural products, and stimulate the majority of cultural and artistic workers to provide the best spiritual food for the people. On the other hand, it is also necessary to refine institutions of public cultural service in urban and rural areas, optimise the allocation of cultural resources in these areas, stimulate the expansion of coverage and enhancement of effectiveness of grassroots cultural projects, and encourage social forces to participate in the construction of institutions for public cultural service.

To this end it is necessary to refine the working mechanisms for the guidance of public opinion which uphold the correct orientation. In this regard it is necessary to firmly uphold unity, stability and encouragement, focus on positive publicity, sing the main melody of the central theme, promote positive energy, ensure correct guidance throughout all aspects of work pertaining to public opinion, ensure implementation in the actions of every worker working in the area of public opinion, and improve the capacity for communication, guidance, influence and credibility of the press and public opinion.

To this end it is necessary to establish and improve institutional mechanisms for cultural creation and production which prioritise social benefits and unify social and economic benefits, as well as guide all kinds of agents of cultural creation to consciously refer to quality, moral character and responsibility, strive to achieve the unity and double harvest of the "Two Benefits", and achieve cultural ideals and values in the midst of benefitting society and the people.

UPHOLDING AND REFINING THE MAJOR INSTITUTIONS FOR LIVELIHOOD PROTECTION IN URBAN AND RURAL AREAS

Upholding and refining the system of urban and rural livelihood protection constitutes a concrete manifestation of the putting into practice of the party's fundamental purpose of serving the people wholeheartedly, and an inevitable choice suited to the transformation of China's major social contradictions and meeting the people's need for a better life.

We must not only firmly grasp the most direct and realistic interests about which the people are most concerned, but also assess our capabilities and act accordingly with all our efforts. We must also pay attention to strengthening the construction of universal, basic and robust livelihood guarantees, as well as continue to innovate in methods of providing public services to meet the multi-level and diversified needs of the people.

In this regard, it is first of all necessary to improve the facilitation mechanisms for employment which is more adequate and of a higher quality. In this regard it is vital to improve public employment services and systems for lifelong training of vocational skills, refine the public employment service systems and key mass employment support systems in urban and rural areas, establish mechanisms to promote entrepreneurship-led employment and multi-channel flexible employment, form a pattern in which the government stimulates entrepreneurship, society supports entrepreneurship, and workers have the courage to start their own businesses, and stimulate the majority of workers to accomplish work of admirable quality and comprehensive professional development.

Secondly, it is necessary to build an educational system which supports lifelong learning for all. In this regard it is vital to comprehensively implement the party's educational policy, promote the integrated development of urban and rural mandatory education, strengthen rural mandatory education, improve safeguard systems of pre-school education, special education and universal high school education, refine the coordinated development mechanisms of vocational and technical education, higher education and continuing education, support and standardise private education and cooperative education, and build a learning society.

Thirdly, it is necessary to refine the social security system covering the whole population. In this regard it is vital to improve the coordinated urban and rural sustainable basic pension insurance system and basic medical insurance system, accelerate the establishment of a national comprehensive system of basic old-age insurance and the implementation of systems for the continuation of social security transfers and for medical treatment in different locations, improve the systems of work for military veterans and their security, and strive to achieve full insurance coverage.

Fourthly, it is necessary to strengthen the institutional guarantees for improving the health of the people. Health is an important indicator of national prosperity and national wealth and strength. In this regard it is vital to maintain a focus on the entire cycle of life and the whole process of health, refine the national health policy, deepen the reform of the medical and health systems, and accelerate the reform of the modern system of hospital management, so that the general public can enjoy fair and accessible, systematic and continuous health services.

UPHOLDING AND REFINING THE MAJOR INSTITUTIONS OF SHARED SOCIAL GOVERNANCE

Upholding and refining the major institutions for shared social governance constitutes an important task in upholding and refining socialism with Chinese characteristics and promoting the modernisation of the national system of governance and governability. The overall goal of this is to refine systems of social governance, led by the party committee and for which the government is responsible, encompassing democratic consultation, social coordination, public participation, protection of the rule of law, and scientific and technological support, as well as to build a community of social governance in which all bear responsibility, play their part and benefit, in order to ensure that people live and work in a state of peace, social stability and order, and to build a more peaceful China.

Solidifying an effective mechanism to correctly handle internal conflicts amongst the people under the new situation is the key to maintaining social stability and unity. In this regard it is necessary to uphold and develop the new era of the "Fenqiao Experience", unclog and standardise the channels for the expression of the people's demands, the alignment of their interests, and the protection of rights and interests, refine the petitioning system and the comprehensive mechanism for the prevention, mediation and resolution of diverse social conflicts and disputes, and strive to resolve conflicts at the grassroots level.

Refining systems for public security and crime prevention and control constitutes a basic project to improve the ability to manage the public security situation under conditions which are dynamic and characterised by the informatisation of society. In this regard it is necessary to persist in the integration of special groups, mass prevention and mass treatment, and thereby weave together the dragnet of public security, as well as improve the level of mainstreaming, legalisation, and intellectualisation of public security and enhance the integrity, synergy, and accuracy of public security and crime prevention and control.

Improving institutional mechanisms for public security is connected with the overall situation of reform, development and stability. In this regard it is necessary to refine and implement systems of responsibility for safe production and management, improve systems for detecting risks to public safety and preventing and controlling security risks, and improve mechanisms for risk prevention and resolution. It is also necessary to build an emergency management system which is under unified command, specialised, permanent, responsive, and characterised by firm linkages between central and local bodies, and thereby comprehensively improve the capability and level of emergency management.

Building a new pattern of social governance at the grassroots level is the foundation and focus of social governance in China. In this regard it is necessary to stimulate social governance and the focus of service to be orientated towards the grassroots, ensure that more resources, services, and management filter down to the grassroots, improve urban and rural grassroots governance systems characterised by the integration of party-led autonomy, the rule of law, and moral governance, improve community management and service mechanisms, and better provide accurate and refined services.

Refining the system of national security and maintaining national security is an important aspect of the CPC's governance of China. In this regard it is necessary to uphold a comprehensive concept of national security, maintain the security of the people as the overriding goal, political security as the root, economic security as the foundation, military, scientific and technological, cultural and social security as a guarantee, improve the system of national security, enhance national security capabilities, and resolutely safeguard national sovereignty, security and development interests.

UPHOLDING AND REFINING THE MAJOR INSTITUTIONS OF ECO-CIVILISATION

The construction of eco-civilisation constitutes a thousand-year plan for the sustainable development of the Chinese nation and a strategic arrangement for the great rejuvenation of the Chinese nation. Since the 18th CPC National Congress, the party Central Committee, with Comrade Xi Jinping as the core, has given comprehensive prominence to the modernisation of eco-civilisation, firmly implemented the new concept of development, continuously deepened the reform of the institutions of eco-civilisation, enhanced institutional innovation, and created a new landscape for the construction of eco-civilisation. Practice has proven that the construction of eco-civilisation constitutes a revolutionary change involving production methods, lifestyles and values, which must be guaranteed by a complete, stable and effective system, and efforts should be made to break the institutional barriers that restrict the construction of eco-civilisation.

All elements of the natural ecosystem are intrinsically interdependent, inter-constrained and mutually influential, and the construction of eco-civilisation cannot be treated as a reactive form of symptomatic relief, but rather ecological protection must be enhanced in all aspects, regions and processes, and it is vital to abide by the intrinsic mechanisms and laws of the ecosystem in order to implement comprehensive protection, systematic restoration and comprehensive management. To this end it is necessary to make systematic arrangements for upholding and refining the major institutions of eco-civilisation at the level of the overall scheme of the "Five-sphere Integrated Plan". It is necessary not only to strengthen "strict prevention at the source", uphold the harmonious coexistence of man and nature, uphold the concept of respecting, responding to, and protecting nature, implement the strictest system for the protection of the ecological environment, and ensure robust systems for ecological environmental protection at the source. It is also necessary to enhance "strict control of processes", establish a comprehensive system for the efficient use of resources, improve ecological protection and restoration systems, and build solid barriers for ecological security. Additionally, it is necessary to ensure "severe consequences" [for offenders], establish systems for the evaluation and assessment of the construction of eco-civilisation, promote comprehensive administrative law enforcement for the protection of the ecological environment, strictly enforce the system of responsibility for ecological environmental protection, and severely punish acts which damage the ecological environment, holding responsible those whose acts cause serious consequences. Such a comprehensive, holistic, and multi-measured approach, and effectively giving full play to the synergy of the major institutions of eco-civilisation, provides more solid institutional guarantees for building a beautiful China.

UPHOLDING AND REFINING THE MAJOR SYSTEM OF "ONE COUNTRY, TWO SYSTEMS"

"One Country, Two Systems" is the Central Government's basic system for the governance of the two SARs of Hong Kong and Macau, and also constitutes an important system for resolving the Taiwan issue and achieving the peaceful reunification of the motherland. The 22 years since Hong Kong's return to China and the 20 years since Macau's return to China demonstrate that "One Country, Two Systems" is a great innovation of socialism with Chinese characteristics and the best institutional arrangement for Hong Kong and Macau to maintain long-term prosperity and stability.

In order to uphold and refine the important system of "One Country, Two Systems", it is first necessary to fully and accurately understand and implement the principle of "One

Country, Two Systems". Upholding "one country" is the premise and foundation for the implementation of the "two systems", and the two systems are subordinate to, and derived from, one country and unified within one country. No act that challenges the bottom line of "One Country, Two Systems" and no act of secession will be tolerated. At the same time, it is necessary to integrate the upholding of the principle of one country and respect for the differences between the two systems, the maintenance of the Central Government's overall authority over the SARs and the protection of the SARs' high degree of autonomy, as well as making use of the role of the mainland in providing strong backing and the enhancement of the SARs' own competitiveness, and refine the relevant institutions and mechanisms of the SARs based on new practices and needs, so as to uphold and refine "One Country, Two Systems" in practice.

Improving the institutions by which the Central Government exercises full rule over the SARs in accordance with the Constitution and the Basic Law is a fundamental requirement for upholding and refining "One Country, Two Systems". The Constitution and the Basic Law together form the constitutional basis for the political structure, political operation, legal system, and social governance of the SARs, and together they establish the constitutional order of the SARs.

The key to the full and accurate implementation of the principle of "One Country, Two Systems" is governing the SARs in strict accordance with the Constitution and the Basic Law, to establish a sound legal system and enforcement mechanism for the maintenance of national security in the SARs, and to strengthen the system of accountability of the Chief Executives of the SARs to the Central Government. To this end it is vital to resolutely prevent and curb interference by external forces in the affairs of Hong Kong and Macao and their attempts to conduct acts of secession, subversion, infiltration, and sabotage, in order to ensure the long-term stability of Hong Kong and Macao.

Firmly advancing the process of the peaceful reunification of the motherland and completing this great task is an absolute necessity for the great rejuvenation of the Chinese nation. Resolving the Taiwan issue and achieving the complete reunification of the motherland is the common aspiration of all of China's sons and daughters and is in the fundamental interests of the Chinese nation. To this end it is necessary to uphold the centralised and unified leadership of the party on its Taiwan work, give full play to the strengths of socialism with Chinese characteristics, work hard to succeed in Taiwan work in the new era, and firmly promote the process of the peaceful reunification of the motherland.

UPHOLDING AND REFINING THE MAJOR INSTITUTIONS FOR FOREIGN AFFAIRS

Foreign affairs work occupies an extremely important position in the party's overall work of governing the country, and the institutions of foreign affairs work constitute an extremely important part of socialism with Chinese characteristics. Since the 18th CPC National Congress, the party Central Committee, with Comrade Xi Jinping at its core, has taken the initiative to plan and forge ahead, pioneering a new path of major country diplomacy with Chinese characteristics, achieving historic results in foreign affairs.

The world today is undergoing great changes unseen in the past century, and China is at a critical period in the great rejuvenation of the Chinese nation. Under the new situation, upholding and refining the major institutions of foreign affairs work means holding high the banner of peace, development, cooperation and mutual profitability, coordinating the Chinese domestic situation and foreign affairs, coordinating the two major issues of development and security, firmly grasping the central theme of upholding peaceful development and promoting national rejuvenation, safeguarding national sovereignty, security and developmental interests, creating a more favourable international environment for peaceful development, and providing a strong guarantee for achieving the goal of the "Two Centenaries" and the Chinese dream of the great rejuvenation of the Chinese nation.

In the context of upholding and refining the major institutions of foreign affairs work, the most fundamental aspect is to refine the party's institutional mechanisms for leading foreign affairs work and strengthen the centralised and unified leadership of the party Central Committee in foreign affairs work. In this regard it is necessary to ensure that diplomatic power rests with the party Central Committee, thoroughly promote the reform of the institutional mechanisms for foreign affairs, coordinate the foreign relations of the party, the NPC, the government, the CPPCC, the military, localities and civil groups, coordinate all aspects and areas of the work of agencies overseas, and strengthen the party's general overview and coordination of all aspects of foreign affairs to ensure that the major policies and strategic plans of the party Central Committee in foreign affairs are implemented.

As the decision-making and coordinating body for the foreign affairs work of the party Central Committee, the Central Foreign Affairs Commission is responsible for the major work in the field of foreign affairs, specifically for high level execution, overall planning, coordination and integration, comprehensive promotion, and supervision of implementation. General Secretary Xi Jinping, when presiding over the first meeting of the Central Foreign Affairs Commission, stressed that the Commission should play a coordinating role in deliberation and decision-making, promote innovation in diplomatic theory and practice, improve the capabilities regarding orientation, ascertaining the overall situation, and establishing policy, take firm hold of the promotion, inspection and supervision of key works, and provide strong guidance to enable foreign affairs work to continue to break new ground. He also emphasised that under the centralised and unified leadership of the Commission, it is necessary to coordinate and improve local foreign affairs work and promote related work in a targeted and systematic manner by centralised management and rational allocation of local resources based on a global perspective.

UPHOLDING AND REFINING THE MAJOR INSTITUTIONS OF PARTY AND STATE SUPERVISION

The party and state supervisory system constitutes an important institutional guarantee for the party to achieve self-purification, self-improvement, self-innovation and self-development under the conditions of long-term governance. Some of the world's largest and oldest parties have lost power and died, and one of the main causes of this is the neglect and lack of supervision and control. The history of the CPC also demonstrates that when the supervision and control are scientific and effective, then it is possible to detect and solve problems in a timely manner, and when the party's internal political ecology is relatively clear, then the development of the party and of the national cause is relatively smooth. Since the 18th CPC Party Congress, the party Central Committee has promoted the reform of the supervisory system from a political and comprehensive perspective and achieved remarkable results, preliminarily forming the overall framework of the party and state supervisory system.

The Fourth Plenary Session of the 19th CPC Central Committee for the first time clarified the important position of the party and state supervisory system within the system of socialism with Chinese characteristics and the national system of governance, and explicitly put forward the need to improve the party's unified leadership, comprehensive coverage, and authoritative and efficient supervisory system, indicating that the CPC has attained to a new level of understanding of the importance of courageously implementing self-revolution under the conditions of long-term governance.

Upholding and refining the major institutions of party and state supervision involves all levels and types of supervisory bodies and institutions and constitutes a complex piece of institutional engineering. The first and most basic task is to refine the party's internal supervisory system, focusing on enhancing the supervision of senior cadres and major leading cadres at all levels, strengthening political supervision, deepening the reform of the discipline inspection and supervisory system, improving the institutional mechanisms for the supervision of dispatched personnel, and, with internal party supervision as the guiding force, promoting the organic and coherently coordinated supervision of all types of supervision to enhance the overall synergy of supervision. It is also necessary to refine constraint mechanisms for power configurations and operations, uphold legal authority and responsibility, transparency of rights and responsibilities, and unity of authority and responsibility, strictly implement a series of provisions to strengthen supervision, and effectively prevent the abuse of power. In addition, it is also necessary to build an integrated institutional mechanism which deters, disenables, and discourages corruption, persist in unswervingly promoting the fight against corruption, treat both the symptoms and the root cause of corruption, and consolidate and develop a thorough victory in the fight against corruption.

The vitality of a system lies in its manner of execution. Upholding and refining the major institutions of socialism with Chinese characteristics, and even upholding and refining the fundamental and basic institutions of socialism with Chinese characteristics, means not only making efforts for institutional construction and establishing regulations, but even more crucially, to work hard on actual implementation and execution, truly ensuring that firm regulation is executed and injunctions are implemented, and effectively promoting the transformation of institutional advantages into effective governance.

(Originally published in the *Study Times* on 6 December 2019)

CHAPTER EIGHT

CONTRIBUTING TO THE ADVANCEMENT OF THE NATIONAL SYSTEM OF GOVERNANCE AND THE MODERNISATION OF GOVERNANCE

The *Decision of the Central Committee of the CPC on Several Major Issues Concerning Upholding and Refining Socialism with Chinese Characteristics and Promoting the Modernisation of the National System of Governance and Governability*, which was deliberated and adopted at the Fourth Plenary Session of the 19th CPC Central Committee, systematically elaborated the major significance, general requirements, scientific implications, main tasks and practical ways of upholding and improving socialism with Chinese characteristics and promoting the modernisation of the national system of governance and governability. From the perspective of institutional form, it constitutes a scientific answer to the fundamental question regarding the type of socialism with Chinese characteristics which should be established and how it should be upheld and developed in the new era from the institutional form, as well as constituting yet another major theoretical and institutional innovation of landmark significance, which brings together the wisdom of the whole party and has enriched and developed the Marxist doctrine of the state. In-depth study and implementation of the spirit of the Fourth Plenary Session of the 19th CPC Central Committee, is a major political task for the whole party and country.

Socialism with Chinese characteristics constitutes the product of the integration of the basic principles of Marxism with China's concrete reality, is the result of the CPC's role in leading the people to promote theoretical, practical and institutional innovation, and constitutes great innovation in the history of human institutions and civilisation. In the 70 years since the founding of new China, the most fundamental reason why the Chinese nation has been able to usher in a great leap from standing up and getting rich to becoming strong is because the party has led the people to establish and refine socialism with Chinese characteristics, continuously strengthening and improving national governance, with the result that China's national system and national system of governance have gained greater and greater advantages in international competition and have shown great vitality. China's practice fully proves that the Western institutional model is not the only way to govern and modernise a country, but that each country truly can develop its own path. The path to modernisation taken by socialism with Chinese characteristics, including the institutional forms of which it is comprised, has demonstrated to the world the diversity of available paths to modernisation and the richness of human civilisation, and offers realistic inspiration and referential significance for developing countries. In particular, the great success of socialism with Chinese characteristics has led to a new dynamic of the "rise of the East and the decline of the West" in the comparative formation of socialism and capitalism. Compared with "The chaos of the West", "The governance of China" and the CPC's governability it demonstrates have attracted wide attention from all over the world. It can be said that in the history of human civilisation, apart from the case of socialism with Chinese characteristics and its system of national governance, there is no other national system and national system of governance with the capacity, within such a short period of history, to bring about the miracle of rapid economic development and long-term social stability that China has achieved. As we study and implement the spirit of the Fourth Plenary Session of the 19th CPC Central Committee, we must enhance our confidence in socialism with Chinese characteristics and promote the remarkable strengths of China's national system and national system of governance, utilising them more fully.

Socialism with Chinese characteristics is a rigorous and complete scientific system, and the institutions fulfilling the fundamental structural role of the "Four Beams and Eight Pillars" are the fundamental, basic and major institutions. The so-called fundamental institutions are those institutions that reflect the essential content and fundamental characteristics of socialism with Chinese characteristics and reflect the qualitative and prescriptive institutions of socialism with Chinese characteristics and constitute the fundamental basis of statehood. Examples of the fundamental institutions include the system of party leadership, the institution of the NPC, the fundamental institution of Marxism's guiding position in the field of ideology, and the absolute leadership of the party over the PLA.

Examples of the basic institutions include those that embody the nature of socialism in China, define the basic form of the state, and regulate China's political and economic relations, such as the institutions of multi-party cooperation and political consultation under the leadership of the CPC, regional ethnic autonomy, grassroots mass autonomy and the basic socialist economic system.

Major institutions refers to the main institutions in all areas of national governance derived from the fundamental institutions and the basic institutions, such as the main institutions in the fields of the economy, politics, culture, society, eco-civilisation, military, and foreign affairs.

The Fourth Plenary Session of the 19th CPC Central Committee clearly defined socialism with Chinese characteristics as a fundamental, basic, and major system, and upheld the integration of the fundamental, basic, and major institutions. It also united institutional reform and operation, stipulated the fundamental direction of upholding and refining socialism with Chinese characteristics, and put forward important tasks and initiatives to improve systems and enhance institutional execution capabilities from the perspective of reform, development and stability, domestic and foreign affairs, national defence, and party, state and military governance, thereby marking a more systematic, holistic and standardised national system and national system of governance in China.

The leadership of the CPC constitutes the most essential characteristic and the greatest institutional advantage of socialism with Chinese characteristics. In China's national system of governance, the CPC constitutes the highest force of political leadership, and the system of party leadership is the "key" in the system of party and state in all fields and aspects, being the "main beam" amongst the fundamental structural

"Four Beams and Eight Pillars" of socialism with Chinese characteristics and holding the position of coordination, leadership and directorship.

The Fourth Plenary Session of the 19th CPC Central Committee placed upholding and refining the system of party leadership and improving the level of the party's scientific, democratic and legal governance in the primary position in the upholding and refining of socialism with Chinese characteristics and the promotion of the modernisation of the national system of governance and governability, highlighting the leading position of the system of party leadership in the national system and national system of governance. The plenary session elaborated for the first time on the basic elements of upholding and refining the system of party leadership from six aspects, ranging from guiding ideology to major viewpoints to specific measures, all reflecting the requirement of upholding and strengthening the leadership of the party. These new overviews and provisions captured the key and fundamental points of national institutional construction and national governance, and are beneficial for the institutionalisation, concretisation, and standardisation of the party's leadership, ensuring that the leadership of the party is implemented in all areas and aspects of national governance.

As we study and implement the spirit of the Fourth Plenary Session of the 19th CPC Central Committee, we must further deepen our understanding of upholding and strengthening the overall leadership of the party, improve and refine the system of party leadership, enhance the "Four Consciousnesses", entrench the "Four Matters of Confidence", achieve the "Two Safeguards", and consciously maintain a high degree of consistency in the Party Central Committee with Comrade Xi Jinping as the core, in ideology, politics, and action.

(The above is a speech delivered at the First Governance Modernisation Forum and the Eighth China Administrative Reform Forum and was originally published in the *Administrative Reform Insider*, Vol.12, 2019).

CHAPTER NINE

CAPITALISING ON INSTITUTIONAL STRENGTHS AND ADVANCING THE MODERNISATION OF EMERGENCY MANAGEMENT

Over the past 70 years since the founding of new China, the CPC has united and led the Chinese people of all ethnicities to fully capitalise on the political strengths of China's socialist system of being able to concentrate on doing great things, to establish and improve the emergency management system with Chinese characteristics adapted to China's national conditions and has made historic achievements. As a result, China's emergency management capabilities have significantly improved.

We have established the policy of "Vigilance in peacetime and focus on prevention" and clarified the principle of "Integrating prevention and emergency response in normal and extraordinary situations". We have formulated and introduced a series of laws, regulations and rules, such as the

Emergency Response Law, and prepared a large number of emergency response plans, such as the *National Master Plan for Responding to Public Emergencies*, so that emergency management is basically governed by rules and laws. We have preliminarily established an emergency management system with unified leadership, comprehensive coordination, classification by management, hierarchical responsibility, and characterised by decentralised management, and have formed work patterns for emergency management characterised by the role of party committee leadership, government responsibility, multi-party cooperation, and participation from the whole of society.

We continue to promote the work of risk prevention, emergency preparedness, monitoring and early warning, information reporting, decision-making and directorship, coordinated linkage, guidance of public opinion, investigation and evaluation, and recovery and reconstruction, and have preliminarily formed emergency management mechanisms characterised by unified command, responsive sensitivity, coordination and orderliness and highly efficient operation. In accordance with the need for effective response to emergencies under modern complex conditions, we have comprehensively strengthened the construction of emergency response teams, supplies, funding, transportation and communications, as well as public safety awareness education for the whole of society, and significantly raised the level of emergency protection. With an open and cooperative attitude, we have actively participated in international cooperation in the field of disaster prevention, mitigation and relief, established and improved cooperative mechanisms for international disaster prevention, mitigation and relief, and also strengthened the construction of international disaster prevention, mitigation and relief capacities, which has been well received by the international community.

In particular, since the 18th CPC Party Congress, the party Central Committee, with Comrade Xi Jinping as the core, has placed emergency management in a more prominent position, made a series of major decisions and arrangements to comprehensively strengthen emergency management and effectively maintain social stability and national security in the new era, propelled the cause of emergency management in China into a new stage of historical development, and opened up a new realm of emergency management theory and practice with Chinese characteristics.

The first decision was to promote theoretical innovation in emergency management, making "upholding the overall concept of national security" as a basic strategy for upholding and developing socialism with Chinese characteristics in the new era, and further establishing the concept of safe development and the idea of the "supremacy of life and safety first".

The second decision was to promote the reform of the emergency management system, integrate the responsibilities related to emergency management, establish emergency management departments at all levels, promote the comprehensive management of emergency response work, and the optimised management of the entire process of management and emergency power resources, and enhance the systemic, holistic and synergistic nature of the work of emergency management.

The third decision was to promote the formation of legislation for emergency management, formulate and revise laws and regulations such as the *National Security Law*, the *Cybersecurity Law*, the *Work Safety Law*, the *Counter-Terrorism Law* and the *Regulations on Emergency Responses to Work Safety Accidents*, and issue policy documents such as the *Opinions on Promoting Reform and Development in the Field of Work Safety* and the *Opinions on Promoting Reform of the Institutional Mechanisms for Disaster Prevention, Mitigation and Relief*.

The fourth decision, based on national conditions and the characteristics of disasters, was to form a comprehensive national fire and rescue force actively adapted to respond to the rescue needs of "all disasters", and promote the construction of a national emergency rescue system for the new era, in order to accomplish a transformation from being able to handle "single types of disasters" to being able to respond to "all disasters" and "large-scale disasters".

The fifth decision was to develop the international humanitarian spirit, and actively promote international exchanges and cooperation in emergency relief, effectively carry out major cross-border transnational rescue tasks and make positive contributions to building a community of human destiny.

As a result, an emergency management system with Chinese characteristics has now been basically formed and has played an important role in critical incident response.

The *Decision of the Central Committee of the CPC on Several Major Issues Concerning Upholding and Refining Socialism with Chinese Characteristics and Promoting the Modernisation of the National System of Governance and Governability*, deliberated and adopted at the Fourth Plenary Session of the 19th CPC Central Committee, comprehensively answers the major political question of what aspects of China's national system and national system of governance should be upheld, consolidated, refined and developed, and constitutes a Marxist political manifesto and programme of action. Emergency management constitutes an important aspect of the modernisation of the national system of governance and governability and strengthening the emergency management system and emergency management capacity to effectively respond to risk and challenges is an inherent requirement for the promotion of the modernisation of the national system of governance and governability.

The *Decision* makes specific arrangements to improve the institutional mechanisms of public security, with the emphasis on "building an emergency management system which is under unified command, specialised, permanent, responsive, and characterised by firm linkages between central and local bodies, which optimises the construction of a competence system for national emergency management", and provides fundamental guidelines and guides the direction our efforts should take as we comprehensively promote the modernisation of the emergency management system and emergency management capabilities.

We need to study in-depth and implement the major decision and arrangements of the party Central Committee and the Fourth Plenary Session of the 19th CPC Central Committee on emergency management, profoundly grasp the special importance of emergency management in the modernisation of the national system of governance and governability capacity in the new era from the strategic height of achieving the goal of the "Two Centenaries" and the Chinese dream of the great rejuvenation of the Chinese nation, and enhance our sense of mission, responsibility and honour in successfully accomplishing our task.

We should deeply grasp the fact that leadership of the party is the most essential characteristic and greatest strength of socialism with Chinese characteristics, and, under the centralised and unified leadership of the party, promote the reform and development of emergency management, and implement the leadership of the party in all aspects, areas and sectors of emergency management.

We should deeply grasp the significant strengths of China's national system and national system of governance and give full play to the political and organisational strengths of socialism with Chinese characteristics, whereby "when disaster strikes, help comes from all sides, we have a coordinated national response and work with one heart and one mind, concentrating our efforts to accomplish great tasks", and leverage institutional power to address the impact of risks and challenges.

We should closely integrate the actual situation, innovate and develop a system of emergency management with Chinese characteristics, promote theoretical, practical, and institutional innovation in emergency management, take the new path of emergency management with Chinese characteristics, and continuously improve the level of modernisation of China's emergency management system and emergency management capabilities.

We must implement the new requirements of the comprehensive rule of law, adapt to the need for reforms in the institutional mechanisms of emergency management, accelerate the formulation and revision of emergency management laws and regulations, promote the construction of emergency preparedness and standards system, and comprehensively construct the institutional legal system as it pertains to emergency management.

We must strengthen international cooperation and exchange, refine and develop international mechanisms for cooperation in emergency management, effectively relate to the world the story of the establishment of emergency management with Chinese characteristics in the new era, and make positive contributions to jointly building a community of human destiny with universal security.

(The above is an address delivered at the opening ceremony of the China Emergency Management Innovation Forum (2019), and was originally published in the *Journal of China Emergency Management Science*, Vol. 11-12, 2019)

ABOUT ACA

We hope you enjoyed these insights into Chinese socialism.

ALAIN CHARLES ASIA publishes an exciting range of China-focused non-fiction. From the soaring highs and grim lows of China's tumultuous history to the vivid life stories of its major and minor players, ACA has books for anyone eager to learn more about this vast, diverse nation.

To let us know what you thought of this book, or to learn more about the eclectic selection of titles we offer, find us online. If you're as passionate about books as we are, then we'd love to hear your thoughts!

alaincharlesasia.com
@aca_pub